Denial and Distress
Gender, Poverty and Human Rights in Asia

Ranjani K Murthy
Lakshmi Sankaran

ZED Books
LONDON • NEW YORK

Denial and Distress was first published in 1999 by Books *for* Change, Bangalore, India

Published in the rest of the world by ZED Books Ltd, 7 Cynthia Street, London N1 9JF, UK and Room 400, 175 Fifth Avenue, New York, NY 10010 USA in 2003.

Distributed in the USA exclusively by Palgrave, a division of St Martin's Press LLC, 175 Fifth Avenue, New York, NY 10010, USA.

Copyright © Books *for* Change, 1999

Cover designed by Books *for* Change
Pictures courtesy Stan Thekaekara
Printed and bound in India

The right of Ranjani K Murthy and Lakshmi Sankaran to be identified as the authors of this work has been asserted by them in accordance with the Copyright, Designs and Patents Act, 1998.

A catalogue record for this book is available from the British Library.

US CIP data has been applied for.

ISBN: 1 84277 265 1 Pb
ISBN: 1 84277 264 3 Hb

Contents

Preface v

Acknowledgements ix

1. Gender and Poverty:
   Conceptual Issues and Debates 1

2. Poverty in Asia and the CIS:
   Is There a Feminisation? 11

3. Gender Specific Causes
   of Poverty 50

4. Human Rights Violations Against
   Women in the Region 101

5. Emerging Vulnerable Groups
   and Issues: Gender, Poverty
   and Human Rights 119

6. Implications for Policy 145

Annexure 1 152

Annexure 2 155

Glossary 160

Bibliography 161

Preface

Human Development Report 1997 brought out by the UNDP estimates that even after four decades of development, more than a quarter of the people in the developing world live in human poverty,[1] and about a third live on incomes of less than Re One a day (UNDP, 1997). The proportion of women in poverty in the developing world and the extent of feminisation of poverty are contested issues. Yet, there is a consensus that their representation among the poor is more than their share of the population. There is also evidence that poor women experience poverty differently and more intensely than their male counterparts, with certain gender-specific processes leading to these differences. The experience of poverty varies among poor women on the basis of their location or status in other social relations, like race, class, caste, ethnicity and so on.

These findings across the developing world apply to the Asian region as well, where a majority of the poor are located. South Asia, East Asia and South-East Asia have more than 950 million of the 1.3 billion people who are income poor in the developing countries. However, poverty levels have, by and large, decreased in these sub-regions over the last two decades. On the contrary, many of the countries in the Commonwealth of Independent States (CIS) have witnessed a deterioration in poverty trends in the last decade. Income poverty has spread from a small part to a third of their population (UNDP, 1997).[2] Evidence also indicates a gender bias in the incidence and severity of poverty. In fact, if the scanty information on the CIS is anything to go by, the status of women may have declined during the current process of transition.

Will gains in poverty reduction in Asia be sustained over the next decade? Will the countries of the CIS be able to overcome the setbacks in poverty? These remain key questions for those interested in poverty reduction in these two regions. Unfortunately, there are many danger signs.

Economic growth has slumped in many South-East Asian and CIS countries. It has slowed down in some of the South Asian and East Asian countries. Uncontrolled globalisation has increased the vulnerability of the poor to external shocks, as was amply illustrated by the recent South-East/East Asian economic crisis. Some of the developments in the political arena of these countries are also causes of concern. In South Asia, increasing nuclearisation and conflicts between India and Pakistan pose additional problems and they could lead to reduction in resources for poverty alleviation. Religious fundamentalism is also on the rise in this sub-region. Many of the countries falling under the CIS and some of the South-East/South Asian countries are facing ethnic conflicts. After over a decade lost to structural adjustment, on the positive side, international commitment to addressing issues of poverty has resurfaced in the 1990s.

Unlike the debate on poverty in the 1970s, the attention currently being paid to gender concerns in poverty is of a much higher order. UN conferences on women, social development, habitat, environment and human rights have brought issues of poverty, gender and human rights to the forefront.

Realising the need to have an understanding of the symbiosis of local (micro), national (meso) and international (macro) forces – both positive and negative – that have a bearing on the structural causes of poverty, ACTIONAID formulated an ongoing research project, **'The many faces of global poverty as we move into the 21st Century'** (Mukherjee, 1997). It also prepared a three-year Asia Strategy Plan: 1998–2000, which outlined specific strategies to further its intention of *'playing a significant role in the reduction and the ultimate eradication of poverty in Asia'*. To strengthen the mainstreaming of gender concerns in its strategies and activities in the region, ACTIONAID constituted a Regional Gender Working Group (RGWG) in 1996. The RGWG felt that a comprehensive situational analysis on gender and poverty in the region, as well as in the CIS, would be useful to inform its strategy in the region over the next five years. To further this purpose, a study was commissioned with the following objectives:

- to carry out research on gender and poverty in Asia and the CIS, focusing on the sub-regions of South Asia, South-East Asia and East Asia within Asia and the sub-regions of Central Asia, Transcaucasus and the East European Slavic sub-region within the CIS;
- to set up a data base of key regional/sub-regional institutions and resource people;
- to examine human rights issues related to gender at the two regional levels;
- to understand the global factors assisting or constraining poverty eradication and gender equity;
- to identify the critical issues for other meso and macro agencies, especially ACTIONAID in the two regions, now and in the next five years.

The UNDP classification norms on sub-regional groupings of countries have been adopted in this report, with a few modifications (UNDP, 1997: p. 244):

- South Asia includes Afghanistan, Bangladesh, Bhutan, India, Maldives, Nepal, Pakistan and Sri Lanka. However, very little reference has been made in this report to Afghanistan and Maldives; Afghanistan, because little information could be accessed, and Maldives, because poverty levels are low and therefore ratings are fairly high in human development.
- South-East Asia includes Cambodia, Indonesia, People's Democratic Republic of Laos, Malaysia, Myanmar, the Philippines, Singapore, Thailand and Vietnam. Very little reference is made in this report to Singapore where poverty levels are low and the gender-related development index (GDI) values are over 0.700.[3]

- East Asia includes China, Hong Kong (China), Democratic People's Republic of Korea, Republic of Korea and Mongolia. The focus in this report is less on the Korean countries and Hong Kong (China), since they rate well on the GDI (value of over 0.700) and poverty levels are comparatively lower. China is different from the other East Asian countries in many respects, and wherever possible the Chinese experience is highlighted separately.

- The Commonwealth of Independent States include Kazakhstan, Kyrgyzstan, Uzbekistan, Tajikistan and Turkmenistan belonging to the Central Asian sub-region, Armenia, Azerbaijan and Georgia belonging to the Transcaucasus sub-region and Russia, Belarus, Ukraine and Moldova which are distinctly part of the East European Slavic sub-region. The focus in this report is less on Belarus, Russian Federation and Turkmenistan as they score comparatively better on the GDI (with a value of over 0.700). At the same time, focus is not exclusively on the Central Asian sub-region, as poverty levels are high and GDI low in some of the countries falling under the other sub-regions as well.

Though the focus of this study is not on the Pacific region, in some instances sub-regional aggregated data provided by the UNDP reports are included. This data also includes the non priority countries listed above. Though it may have been useful to cull out the sub-regional information on the specific countries of focus, this could not be attempted due to lack of time.

End Notes

1. As per the human poverty index introduced in the report.
2. See UNDP, 1995, 1997, The World Bank, 1990, 1998a.
3. Thailand and Malaysia also score over 0.700 with respect to the GDI, but are included in the analysis since the condition of women in these two countries may deteriorate sharply in the context of the South-East/East Asian economic crisis.

Acknowledgements

We are grateful to ActionAid for commissioning us to do this study. It has given us an opportunity to read a vast amount of literature and put together some conceptual and analytical lessons on gender, poverty and human rights in Asia and the CIS. In particular, we would like to thank members of the RGWG, Asia and the Asia Regional Office, Bangalore, for guiding us through the study, supplying us with in-house material, and encouraging us along the way. Joanna, Abhijit Dasgupta and Bhuvana Krishnan gave us very useful comments on the first draft, which have added value to the report. Sunitha Rangaswami of the Gender Unit, India supplied us with useful contacts in Asia, without which we would have been handicapped.

Representatives of the regional and sub-regional organisations mentioned below responded promptly to our queries through e-mail. We are grateful to each of them. They include:

- Sirporn Skorbanek, Global Alliance Against Trafficking of Women, Thailand.
- Wanee, Friends of Women Foundation, Thailand.
- Michael Chai, Consumers International Regional Office for Asia and Pacific, Thailand.
- Vanessa Griffin, Asia-Pacific Development Centre, Kuala Lumpur.
- Gnanpragasam, Amnesty International, Hong Kong.
- Quann, ActionAid, Vietnam.
- Jake Buller, Canada Fund, Vietnam.
- Vu Thi Yes, SWIF, Vietnam.
- Susanna Hopkins, Oxfam, Vietnam.
- Mika Nakahara, IMADR, Tokyo.
- Sepali, Women in Media Collective, Colombo.
- Shizu, ActionAid, Nepal.
- Dev Raj Dahal, Fes, Nepal.

- Nira Gurung-Burathoki, the International Centre for Integrated Mountain Development, Nepal.
- Hanya Krill, BRAMA, Ukraine.
- Anne Walker, International Women's Tribune Centre, New York.
- Sue Smith, OXFAM, UK.
- Geoff Bernard, Institute of Development Studies, UK.
- Jude Howell, University of East Anglia, Norwich.

We also drew upon the resources and time of many Research Institutions and Documentation Centres: (i) Institute of Rural Management, Anand, (ii) Centre for Education and Documentation, Tata Institute of Social Sciences, Indira Gandhi Institute of Development Studies, AKSHARA and ASPBEA in Mumbai, (iii) Madras Institute of Development Studies, Asian Community Health Action Network, M S Swaminathan Research Foundation and Women in Development Initiatives, Chennai, (iv) Indian Institute of Management, National Institute of Advanced Studies, Institute of Social and Economic Change and MYRADA in Bangalore, and (v) Centre for Women's Development Studies, and Friedrich Ebert Stiftung and PEACE in New Delhi. We are grateful to all of them.

For a short period Shashi, based in Chennai, helped us with the tedious task of making notes and in word processing. We would like to thank her. The domestic help in our homes took care of our day-to-day needs and of our families during this frenzied period. We would like to acknowledge their immense contribution.

The views expressed here are the responsibility of only the authors, and do not necessarily reflect those of the above organisations or individuals.

Ranjani K Murthy
Lakshmi Sankaran

Chapter One

Gender and Poverty: Conceptual Issues and Debates

Poverty as Institutional Exclusion

There is a general consensus that the poor can be defined as those who are deprived of basic human needs. But differences arise on what exactly constitutes these basic needs. Most national governments and international organisations associate poverty with deprivation of basic needs required for physical survival; that is food, nutrition, clothing, shelter, water and basic education. However, the *Human Development Report, 1997*[1] questions such a narrow equation of poverty with the tangible dimensions of deprivation.[2] It argues the need for broadening the definition of poverty to include deprivation in terms of creativity, freedom, dignity, self-esteem and the respect of others (UNDP, 1997). Others, like Chambers (1988), draw attention to a few additional intangible dimensions of deprivation: vulnerability, powerlessness and isolation.

The term 'poverty' here is used to refer to the experience of deprivation of the basic needs required for: i) survival like food, nutrition, clothing, shelter, water and basic education, and ii) security and autonomy regarding stock of food, minimum independent savings to cope with contingencies; control over one's labour, mobility, body and so on. As per this definition, even a women in a non-poor household who is deprived of basic needs required for survival, security and self-esteem due to intra-household inequalities or extreme forms of violence would be considered as poor.[3,4]

There are many views on the causes of poverty as well. The World Bank views the lack of adequate rate of market-led economic growth, labour-intensive employment, and household income as the main causes of poverty (ref. World Bank, 1990, 1998). Such a conceptualisation prioritises market over other institutional mechanisms in meeting basic needs, and views the market as a neutral institution. It also ignores the differential ability of social groups (women, ethnic/religious minorities, dalits, tribals, disabled and landless labourers) to convert income into well-being, and, in particular, of different household members who make claims on household resources on the basis of gender, age and disabilities (Murthy and Rao, 1997).

The *Human Development Report, 1997* expands the analysis of causes of poverty from a narrow concern with growth, employment and household income, to lack of choices, and opportunities.[5] However, it does not make an effort to analyse the underlying causes of this lack of choice and opportunities which can often be traced to lack of customary and legal rights of marginalised sections. Further, it ignores the fact that as important as *availability of choices and opportunities* is the degree to which the poor are *empowered to exercise choices* and *make use of opportunities* in such a manner that their well-being is improved both in the short and long run. Again, social practices and legal rights can at times come in the way of the ability of the poor to exercise choices and make use of opportunities in their favour.[6]

Sen's concept of *'entitlements'* (1981) expands the analysis of the cause of poverty from a narrow definition of income or choices to a broader set of legal and customary rights by which people acquire the means to meet basic needs. Entitlements can be divided into two categories: ownership and exchange entitlements, which are legal and normative in nature (Sen, A K, 1990, Kabeer, 1994a). Ownership entitlements refer to what one is legally or normatively entitled to own, while exchange entitlements refer to what one can exchange (one's endowment) as per law and customary practices. Building upon Sen's framework,[7] the argument could be that in mixed economies (most of the Asian and CIS countries) one is entitled to own productive assets (up to certain limits), physical labour power,[8] and membership in household/community/global society and citizenship in the state one resides in.

The actual endowments,[9] what can be produced using productive endowments (e.g., land, labour) and what can be exchanged for produce and non-productive endowments (e.g., membership in household, community, citizenship), depend on the position within social relations of race, class, caste, gender, ethnicity and religion, and allocation of resources to different social groups within the institutions of household, community, markets (local to global), state and inter-governmental bodies.[10] Interactions within all social relations and institutions contain elements of cooperation and conflict. The different parties or groups (big farmers and landless, men and women, upper caste and dalits, northerners and southerners or a combination of the above,[11] etc.) involved cooperate with each other. However, there is also a strong element of conflict between these groups as to what cooperative arrangement is arrived at, each being more or less consistently better for one party (for e.g., upper class/majority community/upper caste men) than the other (lower class, minority community, lower caste women, for e.g.). On the whole, the poor, and different poverty groups, have weak bargaining power within these social relations and institutions. *Thus the main cause of poverty can be seen as shortfalls in the ownership entitlements, endowments, production and exchange options of the poor and different poverty groups (ref. Figure 1.1), due to their weak bargaining power within existing social relations and institutions*[12] (see Murthy and Rao, 1997 for an elaboration of this framework).

FIGURE 1.1: FAILURES LEADING TO POVERTY
Gender and Poverty: Feminisation of Poverty Debate

Although the rules and practices of these institutions entitle different groups differently and unequally, an institutional approach draws attention to the fact that deprivation is experienced differently

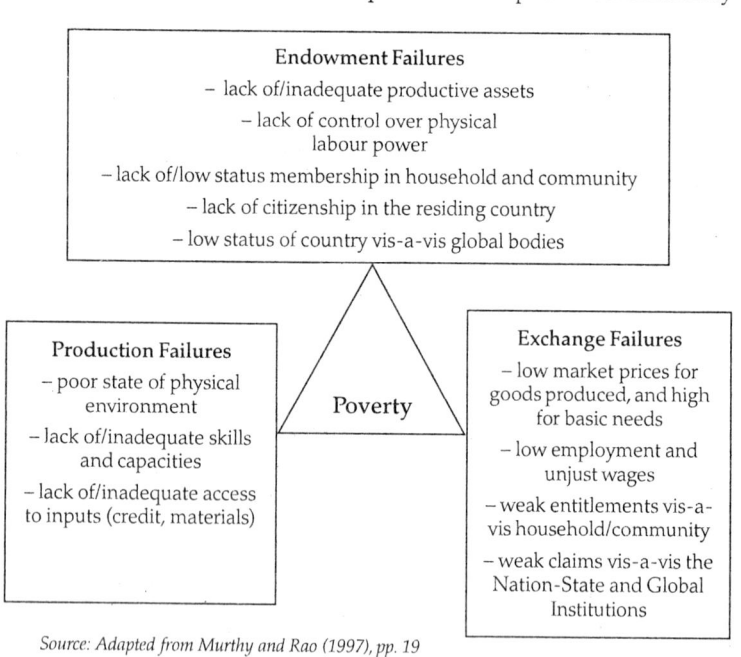

Endowment Failures
- lack of/inadequate productive assets
- lack of control over physical labour power
- lack of/low status membership in household and community
- lack of citizenship in the residing country
- low status of country vis-a-vis global bodies

Production Failures
- poor state of physical environment
- lack of/inadequate skills and capacities
- lack of/inadequate access to inputs (credit, materials)

Poverty

Exchange Failures
- low market prices for goods produced, and high for basic needs
- low employment and unjust wages
- weak entitlements vis-a-vis household/community
- weak claims vis-a-vis the Nation-State and Global Institutions

Source: Adapted from Murthy and Rao (1997), pp. 19

by women and men, girls and boys, tribals and non-tribals, minority and majority communities, dalits and upper castes and so on. Across the world, women occupy an unequal position within different institutions of society, though the extent varies based on norms governing gender and their non-gender related identities. This is reflected in the fact that there is no country in the world wherein the gender development index (GDI) value is higher than the human development index (HDI) value and where the gender empowerment measure (GEM) value exceeds 0.800[13] (leave alone the ideal figure of 1.00). The GDI and GEM figures tell us that women are likely to have lesser access to basic needs required for physical survival than men, and also fewer means to overcome deprivation.

There are no reliable figures on the proportion of women among the global poor. It is frequently asserted that 70 per cent of the world's poor are women (UNDP, 1995 and UN, 1996a). Slightly more modestly, the UNIFEM (1995) states that 'women constitute at least 60 per cent of the world's poor'. No rigorous data is, however, presented to back these claims. The proponents of the argument that poverty is feminised also claim that poverty is experienced more severely by poor women than poor men (i.e., the shortfalls from what is required for survival are often more for women than for men). They put forward the following explanations for the incidence and severity of poverty and its feminisation:[14]

- Female headed households (FHH) are disproportionately represented amongst the poor households. These have a greater proportion of women members than men members.
- Within the households and outside, women and girls have less access to food, education and health care than men and boys. Hence, they may face poverty more severely than men.
- Some of the poverty processes like lack of basic infrastructure and environmental degradation have a more adverse impact on women's work burden than men's, given the former's responsibility to fetch fuel and water, leading to reduced health status.
- Women may also slip into poverty through certain gender-specific processes. For example, given unequal inheritance rights, earning opportunities and returns to labour, women's economic position is highly dependent on men. When their marriage breaks down, women's economic position quite often deteriorates very fast, and they slip into poverty while their husbands remain non-poor.

- Women have lesser means – assets, skills, employment options, education, legal resources, financial resources – to overcome poverty than men, and are more economically insecure and vulnerable in times of crisis. Given greater constraints from the household to the market, their range of income earning options and the returns to their labour and education is lower.

- Women disproportionately bear the burden of structural adjustment in the sense that they are more represented in the growing informal sector, and they constitute a large chunk of the reserve army of labour which is called in and thrown out when necessary. They spend greater time on reproductive work to compensate for cut in social services by the government and increase in prices of basic commodities. In fact, the feminisation of labour seen recently in some of the countries is attributed to feminisation of poverty rather than increase in their mobility and control over their labour.

On the whole, the proponents of feminisation of poverty theory seem not only to be arguing that the incidence of poverty is increasingly severe among women than men, but also that some of the dimensions of women's poverty are different from that of poor men. So are the causes or process of poverty. They are lesser endowed than men, they face lower production possibilities vis-à-vis their endowment, they can exchange their labour for lesser days of employment, at lower wages and more insecure conditions than men. They have lesser access to commodity markets, they can exchange their household and community membership for fewer goods and services, and finally, they are able to stake lesser claims on the state and global institutions than men. Their ability to overcome poverty is much lower.

In the last three years some gender advocates have begun to question the blind belief in the position that poverty is 'feminised' the world over (Lockwood and Baden, 1995, Jackson, 1995, Kabeer,

1997). They are also critical of the instrumental[15] way in which gender has been assimilated into the poverty discourse using this argument, leading to an increase in women's work burden without proportionate increase in benefits. The World Bank's Gender Policy[16] is an often cited example in this regard. According to Naila Kabeer:

Analysis appears to have been replaced in policy by simple and sweeping generalisations (leading to) the automatic inclusion of women in the category of 'vulnerable group', the equation of female headship with poverty, and tenuously substantiated claims about the global feminisation of poverty. This has been accompanied by increased 'instrumentalisation' of women by major agencies such as the World Bank... The conflation of gender concerns with poverty matters allows issues of gender discrimination and injustice which affect the well-being of women to disappear from the agenda. Simultaneously, of course, the poverty of men becomes increasingly sidelined, and the costs of masculinity, whether borne by men themselves or passed on to other family members, is erased from view. (Kabeer, 1997: 2)

Both the sweeping generalisation on feminisation of poverty and its recent critique need to be investigated by ongoing empirical analysis. It is this investigation which the chapters attempt in a limited way within the context of South Asia, South-East Asia (SE Asia), East Asia and the CIS.

Incidence of Poverty in Asia/CIS

The estimates of the number of people living in poverty in Asia vary depending on the criteria used to define and measure poverty, the definition of countries falling under Asia, and the source of data used (Baulch, 1996). The *Human Development Report (HDR), 1997* introduces the human poverty index (HPI) to measure the level of deprivation in basic human development. The variables used in the HPI are the percentage of people expected to die before age 40, the percentage of adults who are illiterate, the overall economic provisioning in terms of percentage of people without access to health services and safe water, and the percentage of underweight children under five (UNDP, 1997). Thus, unlike 'income poverty'[1] measures, which assume that household income is automatically translated into well-being of the members, the HPI seeks to capture the well-being of populations more directly. It is also an improvement over the HDI introduced earlier, as it provides information on a wider range of dimensions of poverty, as well as directly focuses on the incidence of deprivation, rather than average achievements of a country.

Unfortunately, precise information on the proportion of population living in human poverty is provided only for 79 developing countries in the HDR, 1997. Where information on human poverty could not be accessed (like in the case of the CIS countries), information on income poverty and human development will be used to analyse the incidence of poverty in Asia and the CIS.

End Notes

1. Though the foreword to the HDR, 1997 does state that the analysis presented in the report does not necessarily reflect the views of UNDP, if its views were dramatically different, it is highly unlikely that it would publish the same.
2. Such a narrow equation of poverty with material deprivation has been challenged as early as the 1970s when the basic needs approach was popular.
3. A matter of debate within ACTIONAID has been whether women subject to violence should be considered as poor, as they are deprived in the intangible sense (they are more vulnerable, lack little power over themselves and so on). On this issue, the Research Team feels that if the concerned woman also faces tangible forms of deprivation at the same time, either as a consequence or from domestic violence or because she comes from a poor family she could be considered poor. On the other hand, it would not consider a woman who is not deprived of food, clothing, shelter, etc. as poor, even if she is subject to domestic violence.
4. Using this definition, women from *non-poor households* (for example, in north-west India), who are deprived of access to basic needs because of very marked intra-household inequalities in distribution of resources would also be considered poor.
5. According to it, poverty of choices and opportunities is more relevant than income poverty as it focuses 'on the causes of poverty and leads to strategies of empowerment and other actions to enhance opportunities for everyone'. (UNDP, 1997: p. 5)
6. For example, credit programmes for poor South Asian women can expand the range of choices and opportunities they have, provided women are able to break social rules or norms

Gender and Poverty: Conceptual Issues and Debates

favouring male control over household credit and barring women from certain production processes and marketing activities.

Even if these barriers are surmounted, their ability to convert increased income in their hands into enhanced well-being depends on their ability to question norms on the unequal distribution of food and nutrition within the family and norms preferring male ownership of property.

7. Sen (1981 and 1990) does not view membership in household and community, and citizenship as ownership entitlements. But these have also been included as membership in household and community providing independent access to resources, irrespective of one's ownership of productive assets and control over one's labour power. Similarly, citizenship does accord one certain (though inadequate) access to government resources and certain privileges in the market place, which may not be enjoyed by illegal migrants from other countries.

8. Bonded labour is legally banned in most Asian and CIS countries.

9. i) How much private or common land one owns or has claims over, ii) whether one is physically able and has control over one's labour power (not bonded to employer), iii) whether one is an orphan or member of a household, and the gender and age, iv) whether one is a member of a community or is displaced from the community due to migration, war, etc., and one's caste, gender, ethnic and religious identity and, v) whether one is a citizen of the country or an illegal migrant from another country; the country one belongs to, and the caste, ethnic, gender and religious identity.

10. While the state of the physical environment does have a role to play in determining productivity of one's assets, this is largely mediated by policies/practices of global institutions, the national state, markets (global to local) and communities, and only partly by natural factors.

11. Upper caste, class, men vs. lower class, caste, women for example.

12. Institutions can be seen as a set of formal and informal rules, norms or behaviour which shape social perceptions of people's needs and roles and lead to certain allocation of resources and power between people. These rules, norms or behaviour are routinised through certain structures and practices (Goetz, 1995, Kabeer, 1994a and 1994b, Uphoff, 1993). Key institutions which have a key bearing on the poor, and different sections of the poor, include the household/family, community, markets, state and inter-governmental/global institutions. Social relations are relations of power, which are socially constructed, rather than biologically determined or God ordained. They can hence be changed. Key social relations which have a bearing on poverty, include relationships based on class, caste, gender, ethnicity, religion and race. Power relations are inherently unequal and lead to unequal distribution of resources, responsibilities and power.

13. The *human development index* measures the average achievements of a country in three basic dimensions of human development: longevity (life expectancy), knowledge (education attainment) and a decent standard of living (real Gross Domestic Product per capita). The *gender-related development index* measures achievements in the same dimensions and variables as the HDI does, but takes account of inequality in achievement between women and men. The greater the gender disparity in basic human development, the lower a country's GDI compared with its HDI. The *gender empowerment measure* indicates whether women are able to actively participate in economic and political life. It thus differs from the GDI, an indicator of gender inequalities in basic capabilities (UNDP, 1997: 14).

14. See Safilios-Rothschild, (1991), Heyzer, (1992, 1993), Bardhan, K, (1993), Heyzer, N, (1994), Sen, G, (1994), Kabeer, (1994), UNDP, (1995), Buvinic and Gupta, (1997), World Bank, (1994a, 1995a), Baulch, (1996).

15. By the term 'instrumental' these researchers are referring to the phenomenon where women are identified not because they need development, but because their involvement is considered important for poverty alleviation (Kabeer, 1997).

16. According to the World Bank 'Improving women's productive capacity can contribute to growth, efficiency and poverty reduction – key development goals everywhere. Investing proportionately more in women than in men – in education, health, family planning, access to land... is thus an important part of development strategy, as well as an act of social justice' (World Bank, 1994: 9).

Chapter Two

Poverty in Asia and the CIS: Is there Feminisation?

Incidence of Poverty in Asia/CIS

The estimates of the number of people living in poverty in Asia vary depending on the criteria used to define and measure poverty, the definition of countries falling under Asia, and the source of data used (Baulch, 1996). The *Human Development Report (HDR), 1997* introduces the human poverty index (HPI) to measure the level of deprivation in basic human development. The variables used in the HPI are the percentage of people expected to die before age 40, the percentage of adults who are illiterate, the overall economic provisioning in terms of percentage of people without access to health services and safe water, and the percentage of underweight children under five (UNDP, 1997). Thus, unlike 'income poverty'[1] measures, which assume that household income is automatically translated into well-being of the members, the HPI seeks to capture the well-being of populations more directly. It is also an improvement over the HDI introduced earlier, as it provides information on a wider range of dimensions of poverty, as well as directly focuses on the incidence of deprivation, rather than average achievements of a country.

Unfortunately, precise information on the proportion of population living in human poverty is provided only for 79 developing countries in the HDR, 1997. Where information on human poverty could not be accessed (like in the case of the CIS countries), information on income poverty and human development will be used to analyse the incidence of poverty in Asia and the CIS.

As mentioned earlier, it is estimated that human poverty affects a quarter of the world population, while income poverty affects a third (UNDP, 1997). Exact data on the proportion of the global human poor in Asia and the CIS countries[2] are not available. But the available information (mainly from the HDR 1997, supplemented in a few cases from other sources) indicates the following patterns and trends in Asia and the CIS:

- *Incidence of poverty in Asia and the Pacific:* Together, South Asia, East Asia, South-East Asia and the Pacific have more than 950 million of the 1.3 billion who are income poor in the developing world (i.e., 73 per cent of the global income poor). Most of the Asian poor live in rural areas, though urban poverty is on the rise. South Asia has the most people affected by human poverty, and also the largest number of people affected by income poverty: Around 39 per cent of the income poor in developing countries (515 million people) are in South Asia, 27 per cent in China alone and seven per cent in the rest of East Asia and South-East Asia and the Pacific. In South-East Asia, a significant number of poor are located in Indonesia and Vietnam.

- *Sub-regional differences in incidence in Asia and the Pacific:* Poverty levels vary between different sub-regions and countries in Asia and the Pacific. Unfortunately, sub-regional level aggregates on population in human poverty were not available. In South Asia, 43 per cent of the population were income poor in 1993. The comparable figure for East Asia, South-East Asia and the Pacific stood at 26 per cent (excluding China, which stood at 14 per cent).

(UNDP, 1997: p.27, Table 2.1). However, this sub-regional level data masks a lot of inter-country variations in poverty levels. In South Asia, human and income poverty are lower in Sri Lanka and Maldives than in the other South Asian countries.[3] In East Asia, human and income poverty levels are higher in China and Mongolia than the other countries, while in South-East Asia, Cambodia, People's Democratic Republic of Laos, Myanmar and Vietnam are poorer than Singapore, Malaysia and Thailand. Human and income poverty levels in Indonesia and the Philippines fall between these two extremes.

- *Incidence of poverty in the Commonwealth of Independent States:* In the case of CIS countries and Eastern Europe – classified as industrial countries – income poverty has spread from about a third of the population over the past decade with 120 million people living below the poverty line (BPL) at $4 a day in 1993–94. However, the level of human development is far better than that of South Asia, East Asia, South-East Asia and the Pacific (see Table 2.2).

- *Sub-regional differences in incidence of poverty in the CIS:* Within the CIS (excluding Armenia and Georgia[4]), income poverty is about 77 per cent in Tajikistan[5], 76 per cent in Kyrgyzstan, 65 per cent in Moldova and 61 per cent in Azerbaijan.[6] These countries also score the lowest in terms of HDI, with Moldova worse off than Kyrgyzstan. Georgia, Armenia, Ukraine and Kazakhstan are the other CIS countries whose HDI value is below 0.700. On the whole, it appears that countries in the Central Asian and Transcaucasus sub-regions of the CIS are more vulnerable to poverty and low levels of human development than the countries in the East European Slavic sub-region. Moldova is, however, an exception to this generalisation.

- *Depth of poverty in Asia, the Pacific and the CIS:* As such, the human and income poverty measures do not project the levels and intensity of poverty. Information on the income poverty gap is provided by the World Bank for some of the countries in the above region. Among the 10 countries for which data were available,[7] poverty was comparatively higher in India, Nepal and the Philippines, and less in Sri Lanka, Malaysia and Turkmenistan (World Bank, 1998).

- *Levels of HDI*: Though the HDI value does not reveal the level of human development of the population in poverty, it does indicate the level of human development of the average population. For South Asia, the average HDI value is 0.459, in East Asia it is 0.652 (East Asia excluding China, 0.881), South-East Asia and the Pacific are similar with 0.672 and CIS and Eastern Europe share the same with 0.760. The data do suggest that poverty is likely to be higher in South Asia than in East Asia, South-East Asia or the CIS. However, available evidence suggests that there may be a rapid decline in human development values in some of the CIS countries, as well as in Indonesia, Thailand and maybe Malaysia in the near future (especially human development of women, the elderly and children). Further, human development in some of the countries in South-East Asia, even now, is below the low figure of 0.5, like in the case of Cambodia, PDR of Laos and Myanmar.

- *Trends in poverty across time:* Trends in poverty vary between Asia and the CIS, as well as the different sub-regions. The CIS countries have seen the greatest deterioration in the past decade in terms of poverty. In contrast, most regions in Asia saw a reduction in income poverty levels during the period 1987 to 1993. The rate of reduction was, however, higher in South-East Asia and East Asia as compared to South Asia (UNDP, 1997, Table 2.1). However the progress in poverty reduction may come to a halt. In fact, poverty levels may increase in Indonesia, Malaysia, Thailand, and Republic of Korea in the light of the economic crisis in South-East Asia and East Asia (ref. Chapter 3).

- *Relationship between income poverty and human poverty:* Income poverty and human poverty do not always go hand in hand. Within Asia and the Pacific, human poverty is higher than income poverty in South Asia,[8] while in East Asia and South-East Asia and the Pacific (excluding China) income poverty is higher than human poverty. If one looks at country level data, China and the Philippines have performed better in reducing human poverty than income poverty, while Thailand, Sri Lanka and Indonesia have performed better in reducing income poverty than human poverty. Given the non-availability of data, a similar comparison is not possible for the CIS countries.

On the whole, the data on HPI and HDI suggest a certain prioritisation[9] with regard to human poverty of the population (Table 2.1).

Prioritisation is likely to vary according to whether absolute numbers of the income-poor or the incidence of human poverty/level of human development is chosen as criteria. In the long term, there may be a marked increase in human poverty in the indicated CIS countries in the coming decade, given the cut in education, health and services and the gender and age differentiated impact (ref. Chapter 3). In South-East Asia, poverty levels in Indonesia, in particular, may increase in the coming years as a consequence of the South-East Asian economic crisis and repeated droughts. It remains to be seen whether human poverty and human development levels reach the levels of the countries listed under Priority 1(ref. table 2.1).

Table 2.1: Prioritisation with regard to Human Poverty

Prioritisation	Incidence of human poverty/levels of human development	Absolute numbers of human poor
Priority 1 (HPI of over 40 per cent or/and HDI of less than 0.5)	South Asia[10]: (except Sri Lanka and Maldives) Cambodia, PDR of Laos and Myanmar; Perhaps Maldives[11] in South Asia Vietnam Parts of Indonesia and the Philippines in South-East Asia China in East Asia Tajikistan and Kyrgyzstan in Central Asia/Azerbaijan, Georgia and Armenia in Transcaucasus sub-region and Moldova from the Slavic sub-region	India China (above 200 million)
Priority 2 (HPI between 30 and 40 per cent, and HDI between 0.5 and 0.65)		Pakistan Bangladesh Indonesia (40–65 Million) Vietnam perhaps Nepal[12] Myanmar Philippines (between 10–20 million)

Source: Incidence of human poverty: UNDP, 1997, Table 1.1, p.21 Incidence of human development: UNDP, 1997, Table 1, pp.146–148. Absolute numbers of human poor: Own calculations[13]

Is there a Feminisation of Poverty?

Though UN reports estimate that 70 per cent of the global poor are women, it is not clear how this estimate is arrived at. None of the UN bodies, World Bank, or national government documents provide disaggregated national level statistics on the proportion of women in income or human poverty (UNDP, 1997, World Bank, 1998, ADB, 1998). This section analyses data on the difference between HDI and GDI and supplements it with findings of a study on the distribution of men and women in poor households in some of the Asian countries, in order to examine the possibility and extent of feminisation of poverty in Asia and the CIS. Using data on GEM and sex ratios, it also comments on the need to address gender inequalities in the two regions, apart from issues of women in poverty.

GDI vs HDI

The Gender Development Index measures achievements in the same dimensions and variables as the HDI does, but it takes into account inequality in achievement between women and men. The greater the gender disparity in basic human development, the lower a country's GDI compared to its HDI. The GDI is simply the HDI discounted, or adjusted downwards, for gender inequality.

Table 2.2: Incidence of Poverty and Number of Poor across Countries

Indices	South Asia	East Asia	East Asia excluding China	South-East Asia and the Pacific	Eastern Europe and the CIS
HDI	0.459	0.652	0.881	0.672	0.760
GDI	0.412	0.626	0.823	0.641	0.749
GEM	0.231	0.474	NA	0.399	NA
HDI–GDI	0.047	0.026	0.058	0.031	0.021
(HDC–GDC) as % age of HDI	10.2%	4%	6.6%	4.6%	2.8%

Source: UNDP, 1997: 224, Table 47. Fifth row based on own calculations.

Table 2.3: Comparison of HDI and GDI across Countries

Country	HDI VAL94	GDI VAL94	HDI-GDI	The extent of discrimination HDI-GDI/HDI. VAL 94 *100
Afghanistan	NI	NI	NI	NI
Korea-D	0.765	NI	NI	NI
Bhutan	0.338	NI	NI	NI
Cambodia	0.348	NI	NI	NI
Armenia	0.651	0.647	0.004	0.614
Moldova	0.612	0.608	0.004	0.654
Tajikistan	0.58	0.575	0.005	0.862
Vietnam	0.557	0.552	0.005	0.898
Uzbekistan	0.662	0.655	0.007	1.057
Georgia	0.637	0.63	0.007	1.099
Kyrgyzstan	0.635	0.628	0.007	1.102
Ukraine	0.689	0.681	0.008	1.161
Azerbaijan	0.636	0.628	0.008	1.258
Myanmar	0.475	0.469	0.006	1.263
China	0.626	0.617	0.009	1.438
Turkmenistan	0.723	0.712	0.011	1.521
Kazakhstan	0.709	0.698	0.011	1.551
Mongolia	0.661	0.65	0.011	1.664
Belarus	0.806	0.792	0.014	1.737
Russian Federation	0.792	0.778	0.014	1.768
Maldives	0.611	0.6	0.011	1.800
Sri Lanka	0.711	0.694	0.017	2.390
Thailand	0.833	0.812	0.021	2.521
PDR of Laos	0.459	0.444	0.015	3.268
Malaysia	0.832	0.782	0.05	3.268
Philippines	0.672	0.65	0.022	3.274
Indonesia	0.668	0.642	0.026	3.892
Singapore	0.90	0.853	0.047	5.222
India	0.446	0.419	0.027	6.054
Hong Kong China	0.94	0.852	0.062	6.596

Korea R	0.89	0.826	0.064	7.191
Nepal	0.347	0.321	0.026	7.493
Bangladesh	0.368	0.339	0.029	7.880
Pakistan	0.445	0.392	0.053	11.910

Source: UNDP, 1997, Table 1 and 2, p. 146 to 151.

A comparison of HDI and GDI values across regions/sub-regions (Table 2.2) and countries respectively (Table 2.3) reveal that:

- *GDI when compared to HDI:* Like the rest of the world, there is no sub-region or country in Asia and Pacific or the CIS region where women fare better than men in terms of human development. The difference between HDI and GDI as a proportion of the HDI is highest in South Asia, and lowest in Eastern Europe and the CIS, with the rest of Asia falling in between. There are, however, substantial variations in the extent of differences in performance with respect to human development and gender-related development across different countries in a sub-region. In South Asia the difference between HDI and GDI as a proportion of HDI is highest for Pakistan, and lowest for Sri Lanka. In East Asia, this difference is lowest in China, and highest in the Republic of Korea. In South-East Asia, this difference is highest in Singapore (then Indonesia) and lowest in Vietnam.

- *Absolute value of GDI in Asia, the Pacific and the CIS:* Absolute value of GDI is highest in East Asia (*excluding* China) and lowest in South Asia (0.823 and 0.374 respectively). The GDI value in CIS (0.749) countries is closer to the East Asian (excluding China) sub-region, and in the South-East Asian sub-region it falls somewhere in between the two extremes (0.641). The GDI value in China at 0.617 is below that of the average South-East Asian sub-region, but much above the South Asian sub-region. The absolute value of GDI is less than an abysmal 0.5 in all South Asian countries other than Sri Lanka and Maldives, as well as Myanmar, the PDR of Laos, and Cambodia (Mae-Khong belt).[14]

This implies that the average women in South Asia and the South-East Asian countries indicated, are likely to face double deprivation: overall achievements in human development are low in these countries, and women's achievements are lower than that of men. Only 3 of the 29 countries in Asia and the CIS score a GDI value of more than 0.800.This underlies the point that substantial progress in human development and gender equality has been made only in a few countries.

- *Difference in GDI and HDI rank:* Ranks measure the performance of the country vis-à-vis the indicator in other countries. The countries whose ranking in terms of GDI is better than that of HDI (i.e., GDI rank is lower than HDI rank) include industrial countries like Belarus, Tajikistan, Ukraine (difference greater than 9) and most of the CIS countries and developing countries like Thailand, Sri Lanka, Malaysia, Mongolia and Vietnam. This indicates that in comparison to other countries with the same level of human development, they have made greater progress in addressing gender inequalities with reference to adult literacy, enrolment and life expectancy. On the other hand, GDI ranks lower than HDI in Hong Kong, Bangladesh, Republic of Korea, Indonesia, Nepal, Pakistan and Singapore. This indicates that in comparison to countries with similar levels of human development, they have made lesser progress to address gender inequalities in these variables. However, it should be noted that most of the gains in the CIS countries in terms of gender equality have been achieved during the communist regime. As we shall see later, many of these gains are eroding in the process of transition.

- *Gender inequality in living conditions and income poverty:* Gender inequalities in living conditions are not always associated with income poverty in Asian countries. For example, income poverty in Vietnam (51 per cent) is higher than Pakistan (12 per cent)[15] by international standards of $1 per day, but it performs better in terms of GDI.[16] Within India, for example, income poverty is fairly low in Punjab and Haryana when compared to Kerala, but they perform worse in terms of GDI. This implies that even at low levels of income, gender inequalities in living conditions can be reduced.

- *Possible future trends with regard to GDI:* Human development among women and children in Thailand, Malaysia, Indonesia, and Republic of Korea may decline as a result of the South-East/East Asian economic crisis (ref. Chapter 3). Of particular concern is the situation of women in Indonesia and northern and north-eastern part of Thailand, where a significant proportion of the population is already in poverty. Poverty levels are in fact expected to double in Indonesia by the end of the century as a result of the economic crisis and due to prolonged drought. Indonesian women are likely to be disproportionately affected due to their responsibility to run the household and the fact that they are concentrated in the urban informal sector and rural agricultural sector (UNDP, 1998).

If the bill on Islamisation of personal laws is passed by the upper house in Pakistan, it could have a detrimental impact on Pakistani women. In the neighbouring Central Asian and other CIS countries, the costs of transition to market-led economy are being borne more by women. They are the first to be retrenched when public sector units are closed down, and they are the most affected when social security systems and basic services are affected. New private sector employers prefer employing men to women, as the costs incurred by the company are lower. The resurgence of patriarchal values with rise in Islamic fundamentalism is an added cause of concern in Central Asia, as well as Azerbaijan in the Transcaucasus sub-region; and may lead to a further decline in women's condition and position. At the same time, these patriarchal values have also ensured that women are not abandoned by their spouses in the context of the economic crisis, unlike in some of the non-Moslem CIS countries.

On the whole, data on the difference between HDI and GDI suggest that human poverty may be disproportionately experienced by women in Asia and the CIS. But the extent of feminisation of human poverty may vary between sub-regions in Asia – highest for South Asia, and lowest for South-East Asia and the Pacific, with East Asia (minus China) falling between these two extremes. Gender disparities in well-being seem to be lower in China than East Asia as a whole, and any other sub-region or country in Asia (with the exception of Myanmar).

Proportion of Females in Poor Households

No macro study exists on the proportion of females in poor households in the Asian region or the CIS. A recent study commissioned by the UN Statistical Division and carried out by the International Food Policy Research Institute analysed data from household surveys to assess the sex distribution of poorer households of 14 developing countries. This included Bangladesh, Pakistan, Indonesia, Nepal, the Philippines and 8 developed countries. In the developing countries, the average female/male ratio in poor households was 11:6. This suggests that poverty may indeed be feminised (Marcoux, 1998). Evidence from Vietnam indicates that 90 per cent of the poor in Vietnam live in rural areas, and women account for 52 per cent of the rural population. It is therefore likely that Vietnamese women are more represented amongst the poor than men (Tran Thi Van Anh and Le Ngoc Hung, 1997).

Remarks on Feminisation of Poverty

The comparison of GDI and HDI, as well as the UN study on gender composition of poor households suggest that poverty is experienced more by women than men and indicate sub-regional variations. However, the UN estimate that 70 per cent[17] of the global poor are women seems high in the context of Asia and the CIS. One may argue that GDI estimates are for the general population, and difference between HDI and GDI values may be more among those living in poverty. But the available evidence suggests that gender disparities do not vary with income, though absolute levels of well-being do (UNDP, 1997, Dreze and Sen, 1996, Filmer et al, 1998). A policy implication is that focussing only on women related to issues of poverty, on the basis of the assumption that they form the bulk of the poor, may simply add to their work burden, as well as divert attention from more deep-rooted gender inequalities and human rights violations against women. Further, it may ignore the gender-specific needs of men in poverty, which has been identified as one of the factors for the increase in suicide rates among male farmers in Andhra Pradesh, South India, as the aftermath of repeated crop failures due to pest attacks.

Number of Poor Women in Asia and the CIS

The distribution of poor women in Asia and the CIS is of course only partly linked to the extent of feminisation of poverty. It is also influenced by the population, incidence of human/income poverty in general and the sex ratio. If one takes all these variables into account, the main difference between the above analysis of women in poverty across sub-regions/countries and the analysis of people in poverty in Table 2.1, is that if one assumes that the cut off point for prioritisation of countries (Priority 2) is a HDI value of 0.65, women in Indonesia, the Philippines, Mongolia and Uzbekistan may need to be focused on, while this may not be true for men. Particular groups among men and women in these countries may, however, be exceptions to this generalisation.

> **Maternal Mortality**
>
> Within Asia and the Pacific, maternal mortality is highest in South Asia (554 per 1,00,000 live births), followed by South-East Asia and the Pacific (447), and least in East Asia (95). Average Maternal Mortality Rates (MMRs) in the CIS and Eastern Europe are lower than that of any Asian sub-region at 63 per 1,00,000 births (UNDP, 1997:60). However, these figures mask a lot of intra-regional variation in MMRs as well as intra-country variations. MMRs range from above 1500 in Nepal and Bhutan to 140 in Sri Lanka within South Asia, and from 130 in the Republic of Korea to 7 in Hong Kong in East Asia (Anubhav, 1997). The MMR in China is 95 per 1,00,000 live births. These figures also do not capture the increase in MMRs in some of the CIS countries (Tajikistan, Turkmenistan, and Uzbekistan) in the aftermath of transition/liberalisation (Khan, 1998). The causes of maternal mortality seem to vary across sub-regions and countries. In South Asia, high levels of anaemia, high fertility rate and low proportion of births attended by trained health personnel seem to be the main reasons. In the CIS countries, the cut in expenditure on health services, soaring prices of food grains, and increase in the work burden of women in the 1990s account for the rise in maternal mortality levels.

Another observation which flows from Table 2.4 is the difference which adjustment for feminisation of poverty makes in the prioritisation of countries. The number of women in poverty in Pakistan and Bangladesh are more or less the same without adjustment, as the lower sex ratio in Pakistan compensates for the slightly higher number of people in human poverty (Table 2.1). When adjustment is made for the degree of feminisation of poverty, the picture does change significantly. The number of poor women in Pakistan may be 1.5 million higher than the number of poor women

Table 2.4: Distribution of Women in Poverty across Sub-Regions

Prioritisation	Incidence of poverty amongst women	Absolute no. of poor women: unadjusted for feminisation (excluding CIS)[18]	Absolute no. of poor women adjusted for feminisation of poverty (excluding CIS)[19]
Priority1[20] GDI of less than 0.5, and HPI of over 40 per cent.	South Asia (except Sri Lanka and Maldives) Cambodia, PDR of Laos, Myanmar of South-East Asia. Parts of Vietnam	India China (above/near 100 million women)	India China (above near 100 million)
Priority2[21] (GDI of between 0.51 to 6.50, or and HPI of between 30 and 40 per cent).	Vietnam, Indonesia and Philippines in South-East Asia. Parts of Thailand (ref. Chapter 2). China and Mongolia in East Asia. Maldives and parts of Sri Lanka Tajikistan, Kyrgyzstan and Uzbekistan in Central Asia/ Azerbaijan, Georgia and Armenia in Transcaucasus sub-region and Moldova from the Slavic sub-region.	Pakistan Bangladesh Indonesia Vietnam Myanmar Philippines (between 6–30 million)	Pakistan Bangladesh Indonesia Vietnam Myanmar Philippines Nepal (between 6–30 million)

Source: Own calculations based on data on:
HPI: UNDP, 1997, Table 1.1; GDI: UNDP, 1997, Table 2; Sex ratio: World Bank, 1997, Table 1.1; Population figures: World Bank, 1998, Table 1.1; Gender-discrimination index: Table 2.2 of this report

in Bangladesh. Nepal is another issue. If one takes a cut off point of six million for placing countries under Priority 2, Nepal does not figure in the list unadjusted for feminisation, but figures in the list when adjustments are made. This analysis augurs for a more systematic calculation of women in human poverty, especially in South Asia (other than Sri Lanka and Maldives).

Women in Poverty: Who are They and Where are They? A Sub-Regional/Country Level Analysis

This sub-section first explores the truth of the common assumption that WHHs are poorer than MHHs in Asia and the CIS. It then identifies other groups vulnerable to poverty amongst women, and identifies where they may be located.

The data from Table 2.4 reveal that the incidence of women-headship varies widely across regions and sub-regions. It is highest in Caribbean (35 per cent), and lowest in South and Central Asia[22] (10 per cent). The average incidence of WHHs in Asia (Western Asia is not the focus of this study), including Central Asia is 16 per cent. Amongst Asian and Central Asian countries falling under the CIS, the incidence of women-headship is highest in Eastern Asia (21 per cent) and least in South Asia and Central Asia (10 per cent). Women Headship falls between these two ranges in South-East Asia.

Table 2.5: Incidence of Women-Headship: A Sub-regional Analysis

Sub-region	Population 1993 (millions)	Average household size	Millions of households	Proportion of households female-headed	Female-headed households (millions)
North Africa	151.7	5.7	26.6	0.13	3.5
Sub-Saharan Africa	530.6	5.1	104.0	0.20	20.8
Eastern Asia	1270.4	3.7	343.4	0.21	72.1
South-East Asia	466.0	4.9	95.1	0.13	12.4

South/ Central Asia	1317.0	5.7	231.1	0.10	23.1
Western Asia	160.5	5.1	31.5	0.12	3.8
Latin America	426.4	4.7	90.7	0.21	19.1
Caribbean	34.8	4.1	8.5	0.35	3.0
Oceania	6.6	4.9	1.3	0.17	0.2
Developing countries	4364.0	(4.7)	932.2	(0.17)	158.0
Developed countries	1163.3	2.8	415.5	0.24	99.7
World	5527.3	(4.1)	1347.7	(0.19)	257.7

Source: Marco (1998)

However, these sub-regional level figures hide a lot of inter-country variations (Annexure 1) in the incidence of women-headship. In South-East Asia, the incidence of women-headship is higher in Vietnam, Cambodia and Thailand than in the Philippines and Indonesia: This is possibly a consequence of war and conflicts (Vietnam and Cambodia) or male migration/sex trafficking (Thailand). In East Asia women headship is highest in the Hong Kong part of China, and least in Mongolia. In South Asia, WHH is noted to be higher in Sri Lanka than other countries due to ethnic strife in the latter. Death of husband through natural processes, desertion, male migration, and male illness are the other reasons cited for women-headship in South Asia (Lingam, 1994). Though exact figures for the CIS countries could not be gathered, available information indicates that the incidence of women-headship is increasing during the process of transition, with women being left behind by husbands in search of jobs, and in worst cases abandoned by their spouses in the light of economic hardship. Abandonment rates are higher in the non-Moslem countries. Single mothers and women living alone, in particular, seem to be in a marginalised position. Thus not only the incidence, but also the cause of women-headship varies across sub-regions and countries, and even within countries and localities. But in most countries, the incidence of women-headship seems to be on the rise.

There are very few empirically backed studies on the issue of whether WHHs are poorer than male headed households (MHHs). The available evidence does not reveal a consistent or simple association with poverty. A study carried out in Mongolia suggests that poverty levels may be higher in WHH than in MHH. On the other hand, a study in the PDR of Laos suggests that the reverse is true, since to address basic needs a WHH manages the resources better than MHH. The picture in Vietnam is more messy, and is perhaps closer to the truth. Studies carried out by ActionAid, OXFAM and Desai in Vietnam suggest that poverty levels are lower amongst WHHs whose spouses have migrated outside in search of good jobs and send remittances regularly, but higher amongst single parent WHHs. It also notes that single parent MHHs are equally poor, but the incidence of male-headship amongst single parents is lower than women-headship. In South Asia, widows, with few assets and living on their own without adult male children are very poor, while those left behind in villages by husbands in search of jobs may not be that poor. This is particularly true of upper-caste women in north-western and north-central India, as caste norms on women's behaviour and the patrilocal system of residence restricts the ability of widows to overcome poverty.

Cutting across developing countries, other studies support the conclusion that there is no simple association between women-headship and poverty. A review carried out of 61 research studies across the developing world on the association between WHH and poverty revealed that 38 found the former over-represented amongst the poor, 15 found poverty associated with certain kinds of women headship, while 8 found no empirical evidence of such association.[23] Some of the studies suggest that specific aspects of deprivation, like lack of access of children to education, is higher amongst WHHs with little income (Buvinic and Gupta, 1997), but not with regard to nutrition. An aspect worth investigating further is whether the incidence of transmission of educational disadvantage to the next generation is higher amongst WHHs.

As there is no simple association of women-headship with poverty, identifying WHHs in a country for all activities may not be the best way of reaching women in poverty, or women in general. One needs to identify which particular groups amongst WHHs are vulnerable to poverty, and in which category of WHHs do children bear educational or other disadvantages. An indicative list is given in Annexure 1 for different countries.

Vulnerable Groups and Spatial/Geographical Location

Considering the low to moderate incidence of women-headship in most Asian and CIS countries and the lack of a consistent link between women-headship and poverty, it is highly likely that a majority of poor women are in MHHs. This section tries to identify poor women, and where they are likely to be located, within different countries in Asia and the CIS. On the whole, in the case of developing countries of Asia falling under Priorities 1 and 2 in Table 2.5, poor men and women are located predominantly in rural areas. The proportion of poor women in rural areas may be higher than the proportion of poor men in rural areas as they are more dependent on agriculture (IFAD, 1995a). The main exception to this generalisation may be the Philippines, wherein a substantial proportion of poor women are in urban areas (World Bank, 1996k). In the case of CIS countries, except in Tajikistan, Kyrgyzstan and Kazakhstan, it appears that poverty is either equally distributed amongst the urban and rural areas, or marginally higher in urban areas. More often in CIS countries, women's age, number of dependent children, employment status and marital status have a greater bearing on poverty, than their spatial (urban–rural) location.

Disaggregating further, among the rural and urban poor women the following vulnerable groups can be identified:

- *Women in landless households, women in marginal and small cultivating households and independent women cultivators:* Amongst rural women, women in landless households, tenants, women in small/marginal farming households and independent women cultivators of marginal/small holdings are, in particular, vulnerable to poverty (Bhattacharya, B and G J, Rani, 1995). A majority of the women workforce in China, Bangladesh, Bhutan, Nepal, India, Pakistan, Cambodia, the PDR of Laos, Vietnam and Myanmar are engaged in agriculture. In the South Asian countries, as well as Indonesia and Thailand, wherein land distribution is skewed, density of population is high, and land reforms have not been successfully implemented, women agricultural labourers from landless households and women in tenant farming households are amongst the poorest. Next comes women working as unpaid workers in marginal and small holdings of their husbands, like in most of South Asia and patrilineal communities of South-East Asia. However, this group may have lesser autonomy than women working as landless labourers, and whether this has an implication on their poverty levels needs to be researched. Marginal and small women farmers cultivating their own plot of land, like in bi-lateral or matrilineal communities in Indonesia, Thailand and the Philippines are likely to be poor, but in a better economic condition than women in patrilineal communities (this aspect has also been little researched). In Vietnam there is very little landlessness.[24] Women in small landholding families constitute an important group in poverty. In the PDR of Laos, 98 per cent of the poor have land, and the land to population ratio is higher. In Mongolia, wherein herding constitutes an important activity, men and women herders with few animals constitute an important proportion of the poor.

- *Women dispossessed of land:* In Vietnam, Cambodia and China there is evidence that some women have lost land rights with privatisation, as land use certifications have been distributed in men's names (Asian Development Bank, 1995a, 1996a, World Bank, 1995d). This loss of land rights has reduced their status from cultivators to unpaid workers on their husbands' fields. Of particular concern is the fact that the loss of land rights has reduced their access to institutional credit. Further, in the event of divorce or disagreements, women's access to land may be eroded.[25]

- *Women bonded labourers:* Women bonded labourers (either they alone are bonded or their entire family is in bondage) constitute another significant group in poverty. Women bonded labourers have very little or no space to choose their work, their wages, and when to work. Their labour is bonded to their employer who may be a big farmer, a small scale handicraft enterprise, owner of a small scale sweatshop or a brothel. Often indebtedness of their family or ancestors to the employer leads to their bondage. The system of bonded labour is widely prevalent in South Asia, but is also present in a more hidden form in other countries. Girl children are also engaged in bonded labour in these countries. As of 1995, the ILO Convention No. 105 pertaining to the abolition of forced labour was yet to be ratified by India, Nepal and Sri Lanka in South Asia, Cambodia, Vietnam, the PDR of Laos, Indonesia and Myanmar in South-East Asia, China, Mongolia and Republic of Korea in East Asia and all the CIS countries except Moldova (World Bank, 1995a, Table A-4).

- *Women from artisanal fishing communities:* Women from artisanal fishing communities constitute one amongst the groups vulnerable to poverty. Their marginalisation stems from the marginalisation of artisanal fishworkers in Asia in general, and from the artisanal women's disadvantaged position within the fisheries sector

(ICSF,1996, 1997, Sharma, 1998). Artisanal fishworkers in Asia have been marginalised with the industrialisation, mechanisation and commercialisation of the fisheries sector, and the spread of acquaculture. These processes have lead to depletion of marine resources in Asia, as well as a decline in the access of artisanal fishworkers to these resources (ref. Chapter 4). The impact has been particularly marked in the coastal areas of South-East Asia, but similar processes have set in South Asia as well.

Asian women fishworkers play a vital role in pre-harvesting (making and mending nets and hooks) and post-harvesting operations (drying, salting, vending, processing). However, they are yet to be given due recognition by national governments and international bodies. They are excluded from harvesting of fish which is a more visible form of work (ICSF, 1997).[26] That this exclusion stems from social factors is apparent when one takes into account that women fishworkers in parts of Asia are engaged in equally difficult activities like pearl-diving, harvesting seaweeds, clam, crab and mussel picking, unloading fish, and even capturing fish. Further, their virtual exclusion from fishing in deep sea makes women dependent on men for access to the catch. With commercialisation of the fisheries sector, women fishworkers are losing access to the catch because of preference of men fishworkers (both artisanal and modern) to sell their catch to large commercial interests.[27] Self-employed women in India and the Philippines involved in fish processing are increasingly being displaced and absorbed by industries as casual labourers. Ice storage systems are displacing women involved in processing in some of the Asian countries (ref. Chapter 3).

- *Women from ethnic minorities and scheduled castes:* In many countries ethnic minorities are poorer than other communities. In Nepal, the Gurunj, Magar, Tamang, Limbu and Rai, as well as aborigines of the Terai, are amongst the poorest. In India and

Nepal, poverty is higher amongst scheduled tribes and scheduled castes/lower castes, than in other groups. However, in terms of education, women from higher castes of Indo-Aryan origin are at times more deprived than women from the lower castes or Tibeto-Burman races in Nepal. In the PDR of Laos, all ethnic minorities are poorer than the ethnic majority groups – the Lao (ADB, 1996). Ethnic minorities are amongst the poorest in Vietnam, and have 40 per cent lower incomes on an average than those of ethnic Vietnamese (ACTIONAID-Vietnam, 1997). They do not speak Vietnamese, have many more children and thus suffer from poor health and live in upland areas with poor infrastructure.[28] Tamil women and men in Northern and Eastern Sri Lanka would constitute another poverty-stricken group due to prolonged ethnic strife, though statistical evidence is unavailable. In the Philippines, it is not so much ethnicity, but the individual's religious identity which has a bearing on poverty. Moslem men and women are generally poorer than women and men from Christian and other communities. In China, minority women are generally poorer than other groups. They are often found in border and backward areas (Jun and Xiaojiang, 1998). However, Chinese women who have migrated to many of the South-East Asian countries may not constitute a group in poverty.

- *Women in human poverty in non-poor households:* The extent of intra-household inequalities in access to food, education and health care in India, Pakistan, Nepal and Bangladesh has led to an ironic situation wherein the male members of the household may not be in human poverty, but the women members are deprived of basic needs essential for survival. While this is true of almost all pockets of these countries,[29] gender disparities are particularly marked in some states, provinces or geographical areas. In India, gender disparities are particularly high in north-western and north-central India, and in particular UP, Punjab and Haryana[30] (Prabhu et al, 1996). Thus, while the average person in Punjab has nearly attained high levels of human development (0.72), the women in Punjab have attained only low levels of human development (0.38). Low levels of human development amongst women are recorded in Haryana as well, though it is rated medium in terms of human development of the population. In the case of UP, the human development of the general population and women are both low, but GDI stands at an abysmal low of 0.06. In Nepal, gender disparities in human development are particularly high in the far western hills and mountains and the central hills (South Asian Centre, 1998). Unlike Punjab and Haryana, the level of human development is also low in these regions. In Pakistan, gender disparities are higher in Baluchistan, North-West Frontier Province and parts of Sind than in the Punjab and the mountainous Northern Areas (ActionAid-Pakistan, 1997).

- *Women in backward, environmentally fragile and remote areas:* Within China, human poverty is more pervasive in remote interior provinces of the western region than the coastal areas. Poverty is particularly marked in the Gobi Desert region of Mongolia, when compared to other regions. Moving on to India in South Asia, income and human poverty levels are higher in the BIMARU belt than in Kerala. In Pakistan, income poverty is highest in rural South Punjab, while in terms of HD indicators, Baluchistan appears to be consistently poor among the other provinces (Ul Haq and Haq, 1998). In Nepal, human poverty is highest in central Terai, followed by central mountains and far western hills, while it is lower in eastern Terai and the central hills (Nepal HDR-1998). The north-eastern and southern parts of Bangladesh are perhaps the poorest. In Thailand, income and human poverty are higher in the north-eastern and northern parts than in the other parts of the country. In the Philippines, nearly half the population below the income poverty line live in upland areas, while the urban poor are concentrated in Luzon. In Vietnam, poverty is higher in northern highlands, north-central coastal strip and central highlands than the southern delta. In the PDR of Laos, poverty is more concentrated in the central region, when compared to the northern and southern parts. In Armenia, the earthquake zones and border areas are the regions affected very badly. Nakhichevan is one of the poorest regions in Azerbaijan, while the south-west region is relatively better off (World Bank, 1997b). In Kyrgyzstan, the poorest population resides in the south of the region along the rural cities of Osh, Naryn, D Jalalabad and Talas. The southern and central parts of Tajikistan – devastated by protracted civil war – are the poorest in the country. In particular, Garm and Kulyab region and Kurgen Teppe in central and southern Tajikistan are particularly affected (Khan, 1998). The Chernobyl victims constitute a significant proportion of the poor in Ukraine.

- *Urban women in the informal sector and internal migrant women:* Though it is true that poverty in most Asian developing countries[31] is still rural, the proportion of poor in urban areas is on the rise. The urban poor comprise people who have been in the city or town for over few generations, as well as those who have recently migrated from rural areas in search of jobs.[32] Data from national statistics indicate that in Indonesia and Sri Lanka, urban poverty is higher than rural poverty. In India and China, the rate of rural poverty has declined at a faster rate than urban poverty between the early 1990s and the mid-1990s (World Bank, 1998: Table 2.7). In China a significant proportion of the urban poor comprise of migrants from rural areas. They are forced to work in lower than average urban wages and live in unsanitary conditions. Jobs like secretaries, hotel clerks, bus drivers and all levels of management are prohibited for the migrants. Some are even forced to enter the sex trade in cities to make both ends meet (Davin, 1996). In contrast to India and China, in Bangladesh urban poverty has declined more rapidly than rural poverty.

- *Urban unskilled women faced with retrenchment in the context of economic crisis/transition:* In parts of South-East/East Asia – Thailand, Indonesia and Korea – urban poverty has been noted to have increased with the recent economic crisis. Casual workers in factories have been laid off, and the first people being asked to leave are predominantly women. Construction workers, workers in the fisheries sector, and taxi drivers in urban areas in Thailand have lost jobs with the collapse of these sectors. Many of them have migrated to rural areas in search of jobs. An increase in conflicts have been noted in urban slums in Thailand, as the poor compete for the scarce number of jobs which are available. Though definitely not as poor as the workers in the informal sector, South-East Asian women in white collar jobs have been the first to be retrenched whenever cost cutting measures are resorted to in industries. This in the long run may also deprive them of opportunities to move up the ladder.[33]

Increase in urban poverty is being transferred to the rural areas in Thailand through reduced money transfers to the elderly relatives living in rural areas and increased in-migration to rural areas. Affected deeply by the crisis, both in urban and rural areas in countries like Thailand, Indonesia, Malaysia and Republic of Korea, poor women have to face the burden of increased inflation, recession, loss of jobs, inflation in prices of commodities, high interest credit and privatisation of social services. Urban poor women feel the pinch more as they have very little scope to meet their consumption needs through subsistence agriculture (DAWN/APDC statement on the South-East Asian crisis, 1998[34]). Retrenchment of women has also been noted in Vietnam with the closure or downsizing of state-owned enterprises. The first to be asked to go are women.[35] It is however, not clear, whether they are unskilled or skilled workers, and whether they are a group in abject poverty, or relative poverty in comparison to the previous situation.

In the CIS, the poor include blue-collar urban workers who have been laid off by industries in the process of transition. In particular, women are the first who are asked to go. This is mainly due to higher costs for employers (maternity leave, etc.), as well as the return of patriarchal ideologies. While educated, white-collared unemployed women professionals may not face absolute poverty, they have experienced a sharp deterioration in their living conditions, leading to high rates of suicide, divorce, alcoholism and domestic violence, especially in the non-Moslem CIS countries (Russia and Ukraine are two examples). One study notes that the reported unemployment figures in Russia may be misleading as some of the workers (women and men) are employed without pay or working for wages on which they cannot afford to live (The Moscow Center for Gender Studies, 1998).

- *Women refugees, internally displaced persons, and those affected by war:* Poverty levels among internally displaced persons, refugees and returnees are often much higher than the average population[36] (Links, 1997). As of January 1997, about 1.5 million persons were of concern to UNHCR in the area covered by the Bureau for Asia and the Pacific. A majority of refugees are women and children, and a significant proportion are Moslems[37] (Wali, 1998). This population comprised 905,000 refugees and asylum seekers, 406,000 returnees and 229,000 internally displaced persons. Of the refugees, the largest caseloads were in China (290,100), India (268,400),[38] Nepal (126,800),[39] Thailand (108,000) and Bangladesh (30,700).[40] The largest assisted returnee caseloads were in Myanmar (219,300), Vietnam (105,600) and Sri Lanka (54,000).[41] Such detailed information could not be accessed for the CIS (UNHCR, 1997).

Internally displaced groups in Armenia, Azerbaijan and Georgia constitute a significant proportion of the poor in these countries. Armenia and Azerbaijan are in conflict over Nagorno-Karbakh, while in Georgia the conflict is over the demand for a separate Abkhazia. Refugees, internally displaced persons and returnees often have lost access to their productive assets, family and kinship support systems, basic needs and can stake lesser claims on state services than the normal population. Further, in times of economic crisis their identity gets blurred with illegal migrants, and they are faced with the threat of being sent back.[42] Women refugees and internally displaced persons are particularly affected, as they depend more than men on kinship and community structures for their survival (Emmott, 1996). They also tend to attach less priority to their needs than the needs of their children and family members, and consequently suffer in terms of their health. Gender bias of development agencies also comes in the way of their ability to access relief and rehabilitation efforts. Women refugees are also subject to other forms of human rights violation (ref. Chapter 4). Apart from refugees and displaced persons, another important group in poverty comprise war widows, wives of those conscripted, wives of handicapped soldiers and women injured through warfare. The sudden loss of the 'breadwinner' or at least another earning family member can change the poverty status of these women and their families. Such women also find it difficult to access basic services and compensatory measures from the government.

- *Women in large families, in young families, elderly women, children, orphans, the disabled:* In the CIS countries, poverty cannot be classified as rural or urban, or located in particular occupational groups. Gender, age and demography seems to have a large bearing on who is in poverty (see *The Moscow Center for Gender Studies,* 1998). Large families seem more vulnerable to poverty than small families, especially those with a lot of dependents.

Women in such families have to manage declining incomes on the one hand, and declining social services on the other. The elderly women and men are another group in poverty, as the absolute values of pensions have declined in the light of inflation. The disabled, especially from poor families, are marginalised in most CIS countries and Asia. In the context of CIS, they also have to cope with the steep decline in availability of social services and security. Children from poor families in some of the former CIS countries are facing educational and nutrition deprivation in the light of user charges and cutting down of state expenditure on social services (Carlson, 1994). In Ukraine, Kyrgyzstan and Tajikistan, child labour – both girls and boys – has been noted to have increased. Children are employed in carpet making, weaving, petty trade and even in mining. A steep increase in child prostitution and pornography has been noted in Ukraine, being adopted as survival strategies.

Variables such as age, physical ability, household size and composition also need to be taken into account in the Asian countries (see Brakel and Anderson, 1998). In the case of countries in conflict/which were in conflict (Vietnam and Cambodia), the disabled and orphans, especially from low income groups, constitute an important section of the poor (Mehta, 1993, Mehmet, 1997). According to a study carried out by the Centre of Women's Labour (MOLISA's), two-thirds of the disabled in Vietnam are living below the poverty line, of whom 60 per cent are women. They have little chance of integrating themselves into the market economy.[43]

Like in the case of the CIS, the poorer households in Asia also tend to have a larger number of dependents. Child labour is a rampant problem in South Asia,[44] but it is also increasing in some of the South-East Asian countries in the light of the economic crisis. For example, an increase in child labour, prostitution and begging has been noted in Thailand in the last two years. Child prostitution is also on the rise in South Asia. With improvements in human development, the number and proportion of the elderly are increasing in most parts of Asia.[45] Virtually all over Asia, except perhaps parts of South Asia, women outlive men due to biological reasons. For example, in China, the Philippines, Indonesia and Vietnam, women on an average outlive men by 3–4 years. Poverty is a major issue among the elderly women from poor families, as well as the abandoned elderly women from affluent families with little assets of their own. They are often an ignored group by policy makers and planners, and not taken into account when user charges are introduced (Sen, G, 1995, Varley, 1998, personal communication with Suzanna Hopkins, Oxfam). The elderly women in Asia now predominantly live in rural areas, but the proportion in urban areas may increase in the coming decade.

- *Low Skilled Women Workers in Export Processing Zones:* Export processing zones (EPZs) were established as early as the 1970s in some of the South-East Asian countries and subsequently spread to South Asian countries as well. It is part of the larger trend towards globalisation and liberalisation of the economy, and used as a strategy for making use of cheap labour in developing countries for enhancing profits. Most of the firms are owned by Transnational Corporations (TNCs) with investors mainly from US, Europe, and the more affluent Asian countries like Hong Kong (China), South Korea and Singapore. Such EPZs are located in the Philippines, Indonesia, Thailand, Malaysia, Sri Lanka, India, and Bangladesh. Women employed by EPZs in the Philippines, Malaysia and Sri Lanka comprise 85–90 per cent (cited in Kumidini Rosa, 1994), and are found in industries such as textiles, electronics, garments and food products. In India and Bangladesh, the percentage of women varies with the industry and the gender-related norms in the place of location (Banerjee,

1997). Though not as marked as in South-East Asia, they still constitute the majority.

Cutting across countries, most of the women were from rural areas, and shared more or less a common profile. They were young, literate, single, often from poor families, and have limited experience in wage employment. A majority of them worked in the lower rungs of the ladder as part of the assembly line, while the supervisory roles were taken by men. In Malaysia, however, few women were found in skilled jobs such as the electronics industry. While unskilled women workers definitely earned more than usual, and gained some amount of freedom from patriarchal structures (in India[46] and Bangladesh for example), in Malayasia they worked under highly exploitative conditions, and were vulnerable to slipping back to poverty in the event of being fired. Their terms were not secure, they worked extremely long hours, lived under unsafe conditions in barrages, were fired upon marriage, and were prohibited from organising themselves. Though they faced a variety of occupational health problems, health facilities were often not provided, and neither was effective legislation in place for compensation. In Thailand, several young women have died of chemical poisoning in the electronics industry (Theobald, 1996). A 'pseudo-culture' of applying make-up, beauty competitions, and Christmas parties was introduced to distract workers from these conditions.

With the South-East Asian/East Asian economic crisis, some of the women employed in these zones have lost their jobs. In spite of restrictions, of late, with a newly emerging consciousness in this relatively recent phase of industrialisation, some women workers have played a central role in organising and demanding for better working conditions. However, for a significant majority, especially from Thailand, there are hardly other viable options, apart from the sex industry.

- *Transnational Unskilled Women Migrant Workers and Migrant Sex Workers:* Transnational migration has increased with globalisation in the 1980s, though it existed earlier as well. Skilled/professional migrants often go through legal channels, and are paid well and hold secure jobs. A large proportion of unskilled workers, however, migrate illegally with false passports, and often take loans from the agent for travel and other purposes (UNDP/ ARTEP, 1993). At times they are not paid the wages agreed upon. Even though they may often earn better wages than back home, by the time they repay the loan it is over a year. Many of them opt to stay back and save some money, but often they are caught by the police for not holding legal documents. Some argue that the agents reveal their identity, as these unskilled workers block their business. Thus, it is by engaging in a risky livelihood option that unskilled transnational migrants try to ward off poverty. Some come back with large savings (compared to their country of origin), while others lose out. But in the event of an economic crisis, they are the first to be sent back.[47]

Women transnational migrants face certain gender specific additional problems. Many of them find employment chiefly in the sex industry (from Thailand in East Asia, Myanmar and earlier the Philippines) or domestic work (Sri Lanka, Indonesia and the Philippines). Many Thai women, especially from the poverty-stricken northern and north-eastern part, migrate illegally to Japan, Republic of Korea and Germany as sex workers.

At the same time, women from Cambodia migrate into the bordering areas of Thailand to engage in sex work. Some are forced into it because of their poverty, while others are duped into it with the promise of some other job. A few educated and professional women, however, migrate to the West to engage in prostitution because of the media myth about life in industrialised countries. While some earn well, they also risk the possibility of contracting AIDS and other diseases. According to the Global Alliance Against Trafficking in Women (GAATW), the SE Asian economic crisis may contribute to more migration and trafficking of women in the region.[48] Others have noted that in the context of recession, women may now have to service more clients to earn the same amount and also face increased competition from local women turning to this occupation for livelihood.

Women domestic workers from Sri Lanka in East Asia and Middle East[49] often migrate through illegal job agents who are not registered, are often not paid the wages agreed upon and are at times subject to sexual exploitation (Women and Media Collective, 1998).

Looking Beyond Poverty: Analysis of the Sex Ratio

A point of concern is that though in terms of absolute levels of human development/deprivation, women in East Asia (excluding China and the Democratic People's Republic of Korea) and the CIS do better than the rest of Asia. Both these areas are seeing a decline in sex ratio between 1970 and 1995, showing a worsening of gender inequalities (Table 2.6). The decline in East Asia is of particular concern, as the sex ratio in this sub-region is now in favour of men (except the Republic of Korea and the Democratic People's Republic of Korea). Though most CIS countries now have a favourable sex ratio, if this decline in sex ratio continues, this position may change. The extent of decline has been particularly marked in the Russian Federation, Belarus, Kyrgyzstan and Ukraine.

With regard to other sub-regions, sex ratio is in favour of men in most countries of South Asia (the exception being Bhutan and Sri Lanka in South Asia). There is a mixed pattern with regard to the South-East Asian countries, with the sex ratio being in favour of men in Malaysia, the Philippines and Singapore, and in favour of women in the other countries. The countries with the lowest and highest sex ratios in the Asian/CIS region – i.e., Pakistan and Bhutan respectively

– both of which are in South Asia. Further, there is a lot of intra-country variations in sex ratios in South Asia as well. Within India for example, sex ratios are below 90 per 100 men in Haryana, Punjab, Uttar Pradesh, Arunachal Pradesh and Nagaland, and above 100 in Kerala (Filmer *et al*, 1998).

Table 2.6: Trends in sex ratio in Asia and the CIS

Country	Women per 100 Men		Change
	1970	1995	
CIS			
Armenia	105	106	+1
Azerbaijan	106	104	-2
Belarus	118	112	-6
Georgia	113	110	-3
Kazakhstan	108	106	-2
Kyrgyzstan	109	104	-5
Moldova		109	-
Russian Federation	120	112	-8
Tajikistan	103	100	-3
Turkmenistan	103	102	-1
Ukraine	121	114	-7
Uzbekistan	105	102	-3
East Asia			
China	94	94	0
Hong Kong, China	97	92	-5
Korea-DPR	105	103	-2
Korea-R	99	99	0
Mongolia	101	98	-3
South Asia			
Afghanistan	95	96	+1
Bangladesh	93	97	+4
Bhutan	99	128	+29

India	93	94	+1
Maldives	89	95	+6
Nepal	97	96	-1
Pakistan	93	92	-1
Sri Lanka	92	100	+8
South-East Asia			
Cambodia	100	108	+8
Indonesia	102	100	-2
PDR of Laos	98	103	+5
Malaysia	98	98	0
Myanmar	100	101	+1
Philippines	99	99	0
Singapore	95	98	+3
Thailand	101	100	-1
Vietnam	106	103	-3

Source: World Bank, 1997, Table 1.1.

The reasons given for the decline in sex ratio in South Asia vary significantly. One group points to the possible under-enumeration of females in the Census data in 1991 due to their invisibility (Srinivasan, 1994). However, given the fact that the women's movement has grown stronger over the decades, and they have made visible women's concerns in data-gathering processes, this viewpoint is quite questionable. A variant of this position points to the possible over-counting of males due to increase in male migration (Rajan et al, 1992).

But the difference between male migration and female migration has not increased rapidly enough to support this position. Others with a greater sensitivity to gender concerns have stressed several gender-specific factors for the decline in sex ratio – i.e., spread of female foeticide and infanticide, sanskritisation and spread of gender biases among dalits and tribals, decline in female labour force participation in certain pockets, increase in violence in certain belts and preference for male protection, spread of family planning and increase in son-preference, increase in dowry across South Asia and rise in costs of the girl child, increase in marriage outside kinship structure and rise in gender bias and so on (Olderburg, 1992; Agnioshotri, 1995). In the case of China, the success of the one child per family population policy is seen as one of the main causes of the decline in sex ratio, through a rise in female infanticide and foeticide (Ramanathan, 1997).

The above analysis of sex ratio, as well as the differences between GDI and HDI across sub-regions, indicate that while poverty in terms of human development is a major problem confronting women in the Priority 1 countries indicated in Table 2.4, the issue of gender inequalities is all pervasive (see analysis of data on GEM in Chapter 3). In no country is the GDI value equal to or above the HDI value. Gender inequalities, if the declining sex ratio is an indirect indicator, seem to be on the rise in many of the East Asian countries, CIS countries, and some of the South-East Asian countries (apart from South Asia) which do not score low in terms of absolute levels of human or gender-related development. Thus it is important to look at not just issues of gender and poverty, but also issues of gender inequalities and human rights violations against women in the two regions.[50] Further, a broader effort to strike at the gender-specific roots of women's poverty (Chapter 3) may be required so that women across the board also derive some benefit.

End Notes

1. A person is income poor if his/her income level is below the poverty line. Many countries have adopted their own income poverty lines to monitor progress to reduce the incidence of poverty. Often the cut off poverty line is defined in terms of having enough income for a specified amount of food. For international comparison (using income poverty), poverty line set at $1 a day is used for most countries.

2. Some of the countries falling under the CIS come under what is popularly called Central Asia (Kyrgyzstan, Kazakhstan, Tajikistan, Turkmenistan and Uzbekistan of the CIS). But this study shall stick to the UN classification which does not separately refer to Central Asia or classify it as part of the Asia and Pacific region.

3. See Wignaraja and Sirivardana, 1998 for a comprehensive analysis of poverty in South Asia.
4. In Armenia and Georgia income poverty level data could not be ascertained.
5. Data gathered by ACTIONAID-Pakistan from Economic Intelligence Unit Reports 1977 is used for Tajikistan (Khan, S A, 1998:5, Figure 2).
6. World Bank, 1997.
7. Kyrgyzstan, Moldova, China, India, Nepal, Pakistan, Sri Lanka, Indonesia, Malaysia and the Philippines.
8. See Ul Haq and Haq, 1998.
9. As income poverty levels do not really reveal well-being of the population, information on HPI and HDI has been used.
10. The percentage of population living in human poverty in India is less than 40%, but HDI is less than 0.5.
11. Data on income or human poverty could not be accessed for Maldives, but HDI value is less than 0.65.
12. Proportion of the population in Nepal in human poverty could not be accessed.
13. Calculated as follows: Population in millions HPI/100. Population figures have been taken from World Bank, 1998, Table 1.1.
14. The high poverty levels in the Mae-Khong sub-region of the PDR of Laos, Cambodia and Myanmar were also stressed by Wanee of Friends of Women in Thailand, which focuses on this belt apart from Thailand.
15. This international poverty estimate for Pakistan, drawn from the *HDR 1997* and the *World Development Indicators 1998,* is lower than the national poverty estimate which stands at 34%.
16. China is ten GDI ranks above Saudi Arabia, even though its real per capita income is one-fifth as high. Thailand outranks Spain in the GDI, even though Thailand's real per capita income is less than half of Spain (UNDP, 1995).
17. For the 70:30 ratio to hold true, a proportion of 233 women per 100 men is required.
18. This figure has been calculated as follows: (population)* (HPI/100)* (Sex Ratio/200). It, however, does not take into account the feminisation of poverty. As data on HPI were not available for the countries of the CIS, it has been excluded.
19. (Population)* (HPI/100)* (Sex Ratio/200)* (100+gender − discrimination index)/100.
20. As per these two criteria, the order of prioritisation of countries falling under Priority 1 is as follows: Nepal, Bhutan, Cambodia, Bangladesh, Pakistan, India, the PDR of Laos, and Myanmar. Parts of Vietnam may also fall under this category.
21. As per the GDI criteria, the order of prioritisation of countries falling under Priority 2 is as follows: Vietnam, Tajikistan, Maldives, Moldova, China, Kyrgyzstan, Azerbaijan, Georgia, Indonesia, Armenia, the Philippines, Mongolia, Uzbekistan.
22. See 'Preface' of this book for details on countries falling under Central Asia, of the CIS.
23. Women in WHH had more autonomy and control over income than women in MHH
24. Only 1.5% of the 10 million farming families have no land. 25% of them have only 3,000 square metres, and not all is arable.

25. Personal communication with Jake Buhler, Canada Fund, Vu Thi Yen, SWIF and Susanna Hopkins, Oxfam, Vietnam.
26. The invisibility of their work leads to women fishworkers' exclusion from government social security measures and bank credit programmes for fishworkers, as is the case in India. On the other hand, they are responsible for repayment of loans taken by artisanal fishing families.
27. Uni-Lever, Kraftfoods and Nestle control significant proportions of the global fishstocks.
28. Correspondence with Sussannah Hopkins, OXFAM/UK, Vietnam. She also notes that what sets them apart from ethnic minority men is their lack of access to education and the sex specific role which they play in child bearing.
29. Except the states of Kerala and Tamil Nadu in India.
30. Based on estimates of Prabhu, et al (1993) on HDI and Prabhu, et al (1996) on GDI, both cited in Prabhu, et al (1996).
31. There are notable exceptions. In Mongolia poverty is equally distributed in urban and rural areas. Urban poor are more deprived than those in rural areas in their access to meat, milk and nutrition.
32. Though some of the Asian economies have experienced growth in agriculture, the labour absorptive capacity of agriculture has come down.
33. Personal communication with Vanessa Griffin, Asia-Pacific Development Centre, 1998.
34. In April 1998, a Women's Round Table Discussion was held on the Economic, Social and Political Impacts of the South-East/East Asian Economic Crisis.
35. Personal communication with Jake Buhler, Manager, Canada Fund and Vu Thi Yen, SWIF.
36. For example, in Azerbaijan, poverty amongst internally displaced persons is 75% when compared to the national figure of 61% (World Bank, 1998).
37. The world over, women and children constitute 80% of refugees (Wali, 1998). Globally, 80% of the total world refugee population are Moslems, of this women and children make up 75% (Wali, 1998). However, in Asia (excluding West Asia), the proportion of Moslem refugees may be smaller.
38. India hosts refugees from almost all the South Asian countries (in particular Bangladesh), as well as from Myanmar.
39. Refugees in Nepal comprise the Tibetan refugees and Bhutani refugees. The former have been well assimilated over the decades and are found in the carpet industry. It is the latter group, having citizenship rights, which is in poverty. They are found in the eastern district of Jhapa (communication with Shizu from ACTIONAID-Nepal).
40. Bangladesh has become home to Rohingya refugees from Myanmar (ACTIONAID, 1998).
41. For greater details refer Chapter 3. Women and Children constitute a significant 80% of refugees and internally displaced persons. Studies have noted the high poverty levels of Tibetan and Bhutanese refugees (of Nepal origin) in Nepal, Burmese refugees in Thailand, and Afghan refugees in Central Asia. Tibetan women in China are discriminated in the fields of health, education and reproductive choice. The highest rate of female illiteracy in China is among Tibetans at 82% (World Bank, 1996, Xiaojiang et al. 1998). Internally displaced Tamilians from Northern and Eastern Sri Lanka in Colombo are yet another group in poverty, majority of whom are women.
42. The most recent example is that of Burmese refugees in Thailand in the wake of the economic crisis (ADB, 1998).

43. Personal communication with Quann, ACTIONAID-Vietnam.
44. See Lanksy, M, 1997, Jafri and Raishad, 1997 and Gathia, J, 1998.
45. In the countries of the CIS, life expectancy has been noted to have come down in recent years.
46. See Nirmala Banerjee (1997).
47. In Thailand there are hundreds and thousands of illegal migrant workers who face threats of repatriation, mainly from Myanmar, the PDR of Laos and Cambodia. Some – both men and women – formed part of Thailand's low paid construction and fisheries workforce before the economic crisis. In Feb. 1998 the government announced the repatriation of 300,000 illegal migrant workers within six months in the light of the economic crisis.
48. Communication with Sirporn Skrobanek, GAATW, Thailand.
49. The Ministry of Labour estimates that there are at present over a million Sri Lankan migrant workers employed overseas. 70% of them are women, especially engaged in domestic work (cited in *Women and Media Collective*, 1988).
50. On the flip side, though the world over women outnumber men as they have a biological advantage, the reason for the highly skewed sex ratio in favour of women in Bhutan (128) also needs further investigation. Are human rights violations against men by the state leading to vast numbers fleeing the country, or is it that there is a gender bias in favour of women?

Chapter Three

Gender Specific Causes of Poverty

Different Forms of Institutional Exclusion Based on Gender

Some of the key gender specific causes of poverty in Asia and the CIS include the gender differences in (Heyzer, 1992):

- Endowments or ownership of assets.
- Kinship pattern.
- Access to credit, inputs and extension services, training etc.
- Access to employment, wages and terms of employment, and bias in division of labour and work burden.
- Access to household, community and state resources: particularly food, education and health.
- Access to public decision-making.
- Legislation.
- Space to organise and claim rights.

These gender specific factors do not operate in isolation. They interlock with other forms of inequalities to keep particular groups of women in a disadvantaged position. Some of these factors may be more relevant in particular sub-regions, countries or communities than others; or at a particular point of time. These complexities are also explored in this section.

Gender Differentials in Land Ownership and in Community and Kinship Patterns

Land ownership and kinship pattern

In much of South Asia, inheritance is patrilineal though personal laws governing property rights grant women some or equal rights to self acquired property and ancestral poverty. This patrilineal kinship structure is accompanied by patrilocal post-marital residence pattern,[1] arranged marriages, the concept of *kanyadhan*, rigid norms against divorce and widow re-marriage. The exception to this generalisation, apart from Bhutan, can be found in the following areas of India and Sri Lanka (Agarwal, 1994):

- *North-East India*: the home of three matrilineal tribal communities: the *Garos, Khasis,* and *Lalungs.*
- *South India*: here the *Nangudi Vellalars* of Tamil Nadu State practised bilateral inheritance, and several other groups practised matrilineal inheritance, including the *Nayars* and *Thiyyas* of Kerala, the *Mappilas* of north Kerala and the Lakshadweep Islands, the *Bants* of south Canara, and the *Phadiyas* and *Chettis* of Wynad district in Kerala.
- *Sri Lanka*: here all the major communities practised bilateral or matrilineal inheritance – the Sinhalese and the Jaffna Tamils were bilateral, and the Moslem 'Moors' were matrilineal.

However, there is evidence that even in some of the matrilineal communities in South Asia, men control women's property, and take most of the key decisions within the family and the community.

In contrast to South Asia, most communities in South-East Asia are characterised by equal rights of inheritance for sons and daughters, bilateral kinship patterns, access to resources by both men and women, options or choice in marital partner, options or choice in marital residence, no great compulsion to remain in the institution of marriage in the face of intense marital conflicts and strong cultural approval of children remaining with their mothers in the event of divorce (Dube, 1998, World Bank, 1995 c,e,f,g,h,i,j). Vietnam was traditionally different from many of these communities since inheritance was traditionally patrilineal and there was a distinct son-preference. During the pre-reform socialist era, women's rights to land improved dramatically, but has again declined during post-reform *doi moi* period. In the process of privatisation, land or user rights have been predominantly given in the name of men. Son-preference continues to persist, and sons are perceived as a means of social and economic security in poor households. Though in Cambodia women traditionally had rights to land, reforms have seen the setting in of a similar process (World Bank, 1995c).

Like in Vietnam, women in pre-revolutionary China did not have rights to land, and land inheritance was patrilineal and the kinship pattern was patrilocal. After the socialist revolution, land redistribution and collectivisation accorded women land rights and transformed the traditional basis for women's subordination in China (Jun and Xiaojiang, 1998). Within communes, land was owned by production teams, with women's access (like everybody else's) governed by the institutional rules and procedures of the rural collectives. The post-Mao government introduced de-collectivisation and a household responsibility or contract farming system, where village work teams divided up the land among existing households (World Bank, 1995d, Kelkar, G, and Yunxian, W, 1997). There are indications that with the introduction of this system, women have lost these rights.

Not much information could be accessed on the traditional land ownership pattern in the countries of the CIS, but in the socialist period, women enjoyed equal rights to land (Lerman et al, 1994). Privatisation of land is yet to take place in some of the countries of the CIS. It is therefore important to ensure that women do not lose the rights gained during the Soviet era.

Relationship between rights to land and poverty

The relationship between land ownership and feminisation of poverty is apparent if we compare the ownership pattern with the difference between the GDI and HDI. The difference is highest in South Asia, and least in South-East Asia, with East Asia falling between these two extremes.

In fact, studies in South Asia have pointed to the overriding bearing which women's independent rights to land has on their well-being and that of their families (Agarwal, 1994). Given the predominantly agrarian nature of South Asian society, land is one of the important means available to the poor to overcome poverty. In general, landless households are poorer than those with marginal and small holdings of land. The latter tend to be more secure in terms of access to food than the former. However, given the gender inequalities in household resource allocation, men's rights to land will render the households less susceptible to poverty. But this will not automatically make women and girl children less vulnerable to poverty. Thus on the ground of women's and children's welfare, there is a strong case for supporting women's rights to land. For groups like widows, deserted women and the elderly single women from low income groups, ownership of land is noted to make the difference between starvation and survival, and enhance their claim-making power with relatives. Women's ownership of land has also been observed to enhance food security and thus reduce theirs and their families' poverty, as they tend to prioritise cultivation of food grains over non-food cash crops.

In capitalist South-East Asia, gender equitable land distribution has been noted to have played an important role in women's improved status – both their condition and their position – in South-East Asia (Dube, 1997). However, there has been little research on the mechanisms through which it influences women's poverty, especially given the absence of marked intra-household inequalities in distribution of resources. Research on gender and poverty in the Philippines has noted the link between globalisation, commercialisation, alienation of land from small farming households, and their pauperisation. Again specific implications of loss of land rights on women's poverty needs to be rescued. Though the loss of rights to land are noted to have led to a decline in the position of women in China and the South-East Asian economies with a history of socialism, the exact impact on poverty of women has not been systematically researched.

Gender Differences in Access to Credit, Water and Extension
Women's access to credit, water and extension

Women's access to institutional credit is much lesser than that of men in much of South Asia, partly because the provision of credit is still linked to the collateral, but also due to gender biases of financial institutions (UNDP, HDR, 1995, Bhattacharya, B and Rani, G, 1995).[2] Their access to credit from moneylenders in the informal sector is also lower due to similar reasons. A World Bank Study on women in agriculture in India notes that though women contribute equally to agriculture and livestock production, they access only 10 per cent of the credit, and form a negligible proportion of the members of marketing cooperatives.

Women across South Asia have very little access to agriculture extension services. Norms against male extension workers interacting with women are strong in Bangladesh, Nepal, Pakistan and northern/north-western parts of India. Women extension workers constitute a small proportion of the extension staff, and do not frequent the villages. They also tend to interact with wives of rich farmers more than farming women from marginalised communities. It is surprising that women's access to credit and extension is also low in communities of Sri Lanka and Bhutan where women traditionally have land rights (World Bank, 1996b,l).

In Vietnam, Cambodia and the PDR of Laos, women have lesser access to credit and extension services than men. In Cambodia and the PDR of Laos, the low level of education among women has been a constraint in expanding women's representation in agricultural extension services. Though there are more than 50,000 women agricultural scientists, extension workers and technicians in Vietnam, they have lower skill levels and training in comparison to their male counterparts. Extension training is usually directed towards men, because of pre-conceptions about women's role in agriculture. New technology often bypasses women because of these ingrained perceptions. The gender profiles of these countries, prepared by the World Bank, confirm that these gender biases exist in the non-agricultural sector as well.

In Thailand, the Philippines, Indonesia and Vietnam, similar gender biases can be found. Many farm women in these countries have been noted to be ill due to lack of knowledge on how to protect themselves from toxic substances in pesticides and insecticides (World Bank, 1996e,k,m,n). On China and Mongolia in East Asia and countries of the CIS, information on women's access to credit and inputs could not be gathered, but it is highly unlikely that the picture is going to be remarkably different.

Women also seem to have very little independent access to water for irrigation. Since most rural Indian women do not own land, their participation in water users' association is minimal, as membership is contingent upon land ownership. Exceptions are those who manage their husband's land in their absence due to migration. The absence of women in the water users' association also leads to prioritisation of water-for-irrigation over water-for-drinking (Ahmed and Krishna, 1998, Zwarteven, M, and Neupanen, 1995). In countries where women have some rights to land and in matrilineal communities in South Asia, it may be worth researching whether they participate more in decision-making on water use and its allocation for different purposes.

Thus, women farmers across the different sub-regions seem to be disadvantaged in terms of their access to credit, water and extension services. The same pattern can be observed analysing the access of women fishworkers, women artisans, and petty traders and women in other marginalised sections.

The linkage between rights to credit, water and extension services and women's poverty

These inputs influence the ability of women to make maximum use of productive assets they own – labour, land and livestock – and produce enough to overcome their poverty (Stephens, 1995). Credit also influences their ability to ward off distress sales of produce or goods they buy and sell, and bargain effectively in the market place and community level institutions. Though, less visible, access to credit influences the ability of the poor to access government programmes (for meeting transport costs, costs of missing out a day's work and so on), and bargain with government institutions. It also enhances their ability to withstand sudden shocks, and access food and health care for themselves and their children in emergencies. Within the family, access to credit increases the bargaining power of women, and influences intra-household allocation of resources in their favour.

However, many of these gains are possible only when access is accompanied by control (Goetz, 1995). NGO experiences in credit in Bangladesh and India indicate that while credit opens an important role in reducing poverty of women, access to credit cannot be automatically equated with control, increase in women's income and well-being. In the case of Sri Lanka and Bhutan, landownership does not seem to be a major determinant of access to credit or extension services.

Gender Division of Labour, Labour Force Participation and Valuation of Women's Work

The prevalent gender division of labour

Across the different sub-regions there is a marked gender-based division of labour with regard to domestic work, child care and the care of the elderly. Largely the responsibility of women is not taken into account in the calculations of the Gross National Product (GNP) and the labour force participation rates of most countries. However, there are some variations in the division of labour across countries. In some of the socialist/former socialist countries in South-East/East Asia (Vietnam, China and Mongolia), men contribute to domestic work and child care to a greater extent than elsewhere, but not to the same extent as women. In a survey carried out in Vietnam in 1997, 30 per cent of the respondents reported that the 'wife' does household work, and only 5 per cent stated that the husband carried out this work. The rest reported that it was equally shared (Than Thi Van Anh and Le Ngoc Hung, 1997).

Cutting across the different regions and sub-regions, there is also a gender-based division of labour in agriculture, industries and services. In South Asian agriculture, in most communities,[3] ploughing, land preparation and sowing are carried out by men, while women (other than those subject to strict norms on purdah) tend to be engaged in weeding and transplanting. Harvesting and threshing are joint activities. Post-harvest processing is predominantly carried out by women. Moslem and upper caste Hindu women (e.g., in Bangladesh) who are not in extreme poverty, may however, not engage in wage labour on other farms. Bulk marketing is essentially a male activity, while women may engage in petty vending.

In most of the South-East Asian countries, while women under normal circumstances do not engage in ploughing and land preparation, in times of crisis this norm is broken. For example, when there was a shortage of men's labour during the war, Cambodian women undertook the task of ploughing. Similarly, in Thailand, while men were away, women did engage in ploughing. In other agricultural activities, there is a more flexible gender-based division of labour in South-East Asia when compared to South Asia. Women's participation in agricultural marketing is also higher than in most parts of South Asia (World Bank, 1996a to h).

In pre-revolutionary China, women were given minor roles in agriculture. But with the founding of the People's Republic of China in 1949 there was a shift in the division of labour. Except land preparation and ploughing, women and men engaged in all agricultural activities. The implication of the recently introduced household contract system on the division of labour is not clear. In Mongolia, where the economy is equally dependent on animal-husbandry, women engage in milking, but there was no clarity on who engages in marketing of milk produce and meat. Very little information could be gathered on the gender division of labour in agriculture, in the CIS countries.

There also appearsto be a marked gender-based division of labour in industries and the service industry. In the CIS countries which are more industrialised than their South Asian or South-East Asian counterparts, there are more women in the lower rungs of the industrial sector in tasks which require less skills, and less in managerial positions. In South Asia, as well as the low/medium human development South-East Asian countries, women in manufacturing and services are predominantly found in the informal rather than formal sector. The exceptions can be found in the EPZs, but even here women are found in low skilled jobs, while the supervisory and managerial functions are handled predominantly by men.

Gender also interlocks with other variables like caste, ethnicity and so on to determine the division of labour between women and men. In Bangalore (India) and Faisalabad (Pakistan) poor women from marginal groups (who are considered polluting) are the ones who are predominantly found in urban waste disposal activities (Beale, 1997 cited in Kabeer, 1997).

Impact of gender division of labour on poverty

The gender-based division of labour has a direct, as well as indirect bearing on poverty. Taking into account both reproductive and productive work, women work for more number of hours than men. On an average, in developing countries women work 13 per cent more than men. The differences range from as little as 8 minutes a day in the Republic of Korea, to two and a half hours in Kyrgyzstan (UNDP, 1995). Women's heavy workload leads to higher levels of ill-health, and gives them less time to recuperate from any health problems. Further, their responsibility for domestic work and child care (coupled with their unpaid productive work) does not give them much time to engage in paid employment, participate in marketing, public meetings and so on, which are some important means to overcome their poverty.

In the workplace the gender-based division of labour also provides scope for differential valuation of work which women and men do, allowing for gender-biases to creep in. Low levels of wages are an important reason why in spite of working for long hours, women engaged in paid work do not earn enough to ensure their survival and that of their families.

Women's participation in the labour force and women in different employment

Given women's domestic work and child care responsibilities, it is not surprising that except in Cambodia, in no other country does the proportion of women in the labour force go beyond 50 per cent (Table 3.1). Close to this comes Vietnam, Mongolia, the PDR of Laos, Democratic People's Republic of Korea, Thailand and most of the CIS countries, where women constitute between 45–49 per cent of the labour force (World Bank, 1998). The lowest labour force participation rate in all the sub-regions is in Pakistan, where women constitute only 27 per cent of the total labour force, closely followed by India (32 per cent).

Women's representation in the labour force is highest in the CIS countries, followed by East Asia and South-East Asia. South Asia on an average has the lowest representation of women in the labour force. Women's participation seems higher in the former/present socialist countries than in the countries which have not had a history of socialism.

Trends in labour force participation rates

However, examining the trends over time, the proportion of women workers in the labour force has come down between 1980 and 1996 in most of the CIS countries (except Armenia and Russia), perhaps signifying the gender-bias in retrenchment practices in these countries. A comparison of trends between 1989 and 1996 may give a clearer picture. In Cambodia, India, Myanmar and Thailand as well, the proportion of women in the labour force has declined slightly during this period. The countries which have experienced an increase in the proportion of women in the labour force between 1980 and 1996 are Sri Lanka, Pakistan and Nepal in South Asia, China, Hong Kong and Republic of Korea in East Asia, Indonesia, the PDR of Laos, Malaysia, the Philippines and Vietnam in South-East Asia. Is the feminisation of labour force in these countries due to increase in poverty or increase in autonomy of women, or a combination of both? What is the impact it has had in reducing gender inequalities?

Link between labour force participation and women's poverty

Women's representation in the labour force seems to have an inverse bearing on the differences between HDI and GDI. The higher their representation, lower the differences between HDI and GDI. At a more micro level, the presence of this link has been argued as early as the 1980s by Dyson and Moore (1983) in their study of the causes of the differences in sex ratio, female infant mortality rates and female autonomy between South India and North-West India. More specifically, women's participation in the labour market (in particular, paid work) increases their bargaining power within the household, and their ability to claim adequate food, nutrition and health care. It may also broaden their horizons and enhance their ability to make claims on community and government institutions to reduce their poverty (Murthi, Guio and Dreze, 1996).

Nature of work and sectoral distribution: a profile

If one analyses the kind of work men and women do (categorised as employers/own account workers, employees, and family workers) across different sub-regions in Asia, some patterns can definitely be discerned. Among the three South Asian countries, women in Bangladesh and Pakistan predominately engage in unpaid family work (Haque, 1998). This was particularly striking in Bangladesh where 83.3 per cent of the women workers are family members. However, in Sri Lanka working women were predominantly employees. In the Republic of Korea in East Asia, Thailand, Malaysia and Singapore in South-East Asia, the patterns were similar to Sri Lanka. However, in the Philippines and Indonesia, over 25 per cent of women workers were own account workers or employers. In Indonesia, however, women family workers outnumbered women working as employers or employees.

An analysis of the distribution of women's work across different sectors – agriculture, industry and services – reveals that a higher proportion of the women workforce engaged in agriculture in the countries of South Asia, China and Democratic People's Republic of Korea in East Asia, Cambodia, the PDR of Laos, Vietnam, Indonesia, Thailand, and Myanmar in South-East Asia, and Tajikistan in the CIS. In Mongolia, Republic of Korea and Hong Kong (China) in East Asia, the Philippines, Singapore, Malaysia in South-East Asia and most of the CIS Countries (other than Tajikistan) there are more women workers in the service sector than in other sectors. Comparatively, a lower proportion of men than woman are found in agriculture in South Asia, East Asia (other than Mongolia) and South-East Asia (other than the Philippines). A greater proportion of men are found in industry than women (except Bangladesh). In the service sector a mixed pattern is observed. The proportion of men outnumbers the women in the service sector in South Asian countries, while the reverse is true in the CIS.

Irrespective of the nature and sectoral areas in which they work, women are predominantly found in the informal sector in South Asia, China and Mongolia in East Asia, and Indonesia, the Philippines, Vietnam, Cambodia and the PDR of Laos in South-East Asia.

Link between the nature of productive work/sector of work and poverty

A comparison of the sub-regions/countries in which women are predominantly engaged in unpaid work and the absolute levels of GDI and gender disparities suggest the possibility of gender inequalities being higher in those countries where more women are family workers, than in those countries where women work as employees or on their own account. This factor, in fact, may be more important than absolute levels of labour force participation rates, as the cash contribution of women has a greater bearing on the bargaining power within the household, than their free contribution in terms of productive labour to household enterprises.

The distribution of women across different sectors also has an indirect impact on women's well-being. If one analyses the growth rates of different sectors between 1965–96, one finds that the rate of growth in agriculture has been lower than that of the other sectors in all the countries on which data was available[6] (*World Bank, 1998*, Table 1.4). Except in the Philippines and the Republic of Korea, women are predominately located in the sectors which are not growing very fast. This fact is more true for women than men, except in these two countries (data on growth rates in the CIS countries across different sectors could not be obtained). Women's presence in low growth sectors implies that the incomes they earn, or contribute to, is likely to be lower than that of men. This could add to the socio-cultural devaluation of women in South Asia.

The presence of women predominantly in the informal sector in Priorities 1 and 2 countries is another point of concern. In instances of recession, the informal sector is the worst hit, and thus women's livelihoods are highly vulnerable to the vagaries of the market. The impact of the South-East Asian/East Asian economic crisis is one such example.

Valuation of work: a profile

If one analyses the valuation of the work of women and men, in all the countries on which data is available, women's work fetches lesser wages than men's work (ranging from an estimated half in Bangladesh to 77 per cent in the PDR of Laos – World Bank, 1996a–l). Part of the disparity may be attributed to differences in skill/ education/energy levels required for the tasks which men and women do, but a substantial part is also due to the gender-based allocation of tasks and different ways in which the work of women and men are valued as per the prevalent legal and socio-cultural norms. Moldova, Vietnam, Cambodia, the PDR of Laos, Malaysia, Singapore, Thailand, Myanmar, Bangladesh and Pakistan have not notified equal pay for equal work (Meng, 1996, World Bank, 1995). In the Philippines, despite higher education of women than men and legal provisions guaranteeing equality, gender inequalities in the labour market persist (World Bank, 1995h). A rigorous study of the skills/energy required to undertake different tasks would be useful to distinguish the contribution of skill differences and gender discrimination to wage differentials in different country and community contexts.

Moving on to the percentage of women's contribution to family income, in no country do women bring in cash income equal to that of men within the family, though their contribution in terms of total working hours is significantly more. Women bring over 40 per cent income in Vietnam, Armenia, Moldova, Belarus, Russia and the Ukraine in the CIS (predominantly, the non Moslem countries). The PDR of Laos in South-East Asia, China and Mongolia in East Asia and most of the CIS countries follow closely. Women's contribution seems to be the least in Pakistan, closely followed by

Table 3.1: Female Labour Force Participation, Structure of Work, and Income Contribution

Country	Earned Income Share (%) 1994 Fem.	Earned Income Share (%) 1994 Male	Female % of Labour force 1996	Female % of economically active population 1994[4] Employer	Female % of economically active population 1994[4] Empolyee	Female % of economically active population 1994[4] Family worker	Female % of economically active population 1994[5] Agriculture	Female % of economically active population 1994[5] Industry	Female % of economically active population 1994[5] Services
Armenia	40.3	59.7	48	NI	NI	NI	11	39	51
Azerbaijan	36.8	63.2	44	NI	NI	NI	36	21	43
Belarus	41.6	58.4	49	NI	NI	NI	13	36	51
Georgia	39.3	60.7	46	NI	NI	NI	24	23	52
Kazakhstan	39.2	60.8	47	NI	NI	NI	15	25	60
Kyrgyzstan	39.5	60.5	47	NI	NI	NI	28	23	50
Moldova	41.4	58.6	49	NI	NI	NI	28	26	46
Russian Federation	41.3	58.7	49	NI	NI	NI	10	35	56
Tajikistan	36.4	63.6	44	NI	NI	NI	45	17	37
Turkmenistan	38.2	61.8	45	NI	NI	NI	41	14	44
Ukraine	41.4	58.6	49	NI	NI	NI	16	34	50
Uzbekistan	39.0	61.0	46	NI	NI	NI	35	19	45
Afghanistan			NI	NI	NI	NI	NI	NI	NI
China	38.1	61.9	45	NI	NI	NI	76	13	11
Hong Kong,China	27.1	72.9	37	3.2	92.9	2.0	1	33	66

Korea-D	-	-	45	NI	NI	NI	42	23	35
Korea-R	27.7	72.3	41	18.4	56.3	23.0	17	25	56
Mongolia	39.2	60.8	46	NI	NI	NI	30	22	48
Bangladesh	23.1	76.9	42	6.4	5.2	83.3	74	19	7
Bhutan	-	-	NI	NI	NI	NI	NI	NI	NI
India	25.7	74.3	32	NI	NI	NI	74	15	11
Maldives	35.4	64.6	NI	NI	NI	NI	NI	NI	NI
Nepal	33.0	67.0	40	NI	NI	NI	98	0	2
Pakistan	20.8	79.2	27	13.0	22.6	47.6	72	13	15
Sri Lanka	34.5	65.5	35	14.9	51.8	12.0	32	17	27
Cambodia	-	-	53	NI	NI	NI	78	8	14
Indonesia	32.9	67.1	40	28.7	24.0	44.7	56	13	31
PDR of Laos	39.9	60.1	47	NI	NI	NI	81	5	14
Malaysia	30.2	69.8	37	13.7	71.5	14.8	26	23	52
Myanmar	36.6	63.4	43	NI	NI	NI	78	9	14
Philippines	30.7	69.3	37	30.4	40.8	19.3	31	14	56
Singapore	30.7	69.3	38	5.1	90.3	1.8	0	30	68
Thailand	37.2	62.8	46	22.6	35.4	29.4	38	19	31
Vietnam	42.3	57.7	49	NI	NI	NI	73	11	16

Source: UNDP, 1997, Table 2 and World Bank, 1998, Tables 2.3, 2.4 and 2.5

Bangladesh and India in South Asia and the Republic of Korea and Hong Kong (China) in East Asia. The other countries fall in between the extremes.

Link between valuation of women's work and their poverty

As already mentioned, lower wages for women imply that they have less direct means to reduce their experience of poverty. Gender disparities in wages also reduce the ability of women to negotiate for equal share of food, nutrition and health expenditure within the household. Women's contribution to family income is determined partly by wage levels, and, in addition, by a combination of their participation rate in paid employment or own account work. An analysis of the data on their contribution to family income and the difference between HDI and GDI as a proportion of HDI, suggest that these two variables may be interlinked. Gender differentials in well-being are particularly high in those sub-regions/countries where women's contribution is low and vice versa. The more women contribute, the greater their bargaining power within the household, and perhaps even outside.

Access to Public and Household Decision-Making: Gender Differences

Access to public decision-making: a profile

Gender differences in public decision-making are partly reflected in the Gender Empowerment Measure (GEM). This measure captures women's access to economic and political decision-making.[7] Data on the GEM could not be accessed for the CIS countries. The average GEM index for South Asia is the lowest at 0.231, and highest for East Asia at 0.474 (global average being 0.418). The GEM index for South-East Asia and the Pacific stands at 0.399 (Table 3.2). However, the proportion of women administrators, managers, professional and technical workers is higher in South-East Asia and the Pacific when compared to East Asia. East Asia scores much better on the representation of women in the Parliament.

Further, the above sub-regional aggregation masks a lot of intra-regional variations. For example, among the South-East Asian low and medium human development countries,[8] the GEM value is highest in the Philippines (0.459), followed by Thailand (0.417), and lowest in Indonesia (0.375). In East Asia, the GEM value in China (0.481) is significantly higher than that of Mongolia (0.302). In South Asia, the GEM value is highest in Maldives (0.33), and lowest in Pakistan at (0.189). Even in Bhutan, with a sex ratio in favour of women, they are hardly present in governmental bodies (Buringa and Tshering, 1992).[9]

Though data on GEM index for the CIS countries could not be accessed, the information available indicates that when reservations were in place for women during the socialist era, they constituted a significant proportion of parliamentarians and the bureaucracy. Subsequently their representation has come down significantly. Women now constitute 4.1 per cent of those at the ministerial level, and 3.9 per cent at the sub-ministerial level of the government (UNDP, 1997, Table 47).

A point of concern in some of the former command-oriented socialist countries of Asia is that the introduction of multiparty elections has led to a decline in women's political participation. In Mongolia, women's representation in Parliament declined from 25 per cent in 1990 to less than 4 per cent in 1992 when multiparty elections were introduced (Asian Development Bank, 1995b). In Cambodia, women's representation in the National Assembly fell from around 18 per cent to less than 5 per cent between 1988 and 1993 when elections were held (Asian Development Bank, 1996a). Though Vietnam has not switched over to a multiparty electoral system, the onset of economic reforms has surprisingly led to a decline in women's political participation. Women's representation in the National Assembly declined from 32.2 per cent in 1975 to 18.5 per cent in 1992 (Asian Development Bank, 1995a).

Implications for women's poverty

Women's participation in public decision-making processes is both a value by itself, and may be instrumental to further pro-women, and perhaps even pro-poor policies and legislation. Women are more concerned than men about the well-being of the population, given their socially sanctioned role to sustain life and livelihoods. If one analyses data on GEM for Asian countries, there appears to be a relationship between the GEM value and the gender-gaps in human development (difference between HDI and GDI as a proportion of HDI), and to some extent even absolute levels of human development. In South Asia where GEM value is the lowest, the gender gap in human development is the highest, and the human development index of the population is the lowest. In East Asia where GEM value is the highest, the gender gap in human development is the lowest. However, GEM value would decrease and the gender gap would increase substantially in East Asia if one excluded China. China seems to perform better than the other countries in the sub-region with regard to this measure. Many of the gains made during the socialist era in the CIS countries have been partly attributed to the high representation of women in public decision-making. Whether these gains will be sustained in the context of the drastic decline in their participation in the process of transition remains to be seen.

Access to household decision-making: a profile

In Asia, women's rights to decision-making within the family and community has varied with the kinship and inheritance systems, marriage and so on (Agarwal, B, 1997). In the bi-lateral and matrilineal inheritance systems and bilocal residence system, women have participated more in decision-making than in patrilocal and patrilineal systems. As already discussed in capitalist South-East Asia, both systems are equally prevalent, and in no way related to the dominant religion. In some of the former command-oriented South-

East Asian and East Asian economies, de-collectivisation of agriculture has led to a loss of women's rights to land. The implications of this on women's intra-household decision-making need to be studied. In much of South Asia (which is patrilineal and patrilocal) men have had greater say in intra-household decision-making. In particular, young women, widowed women, unmarried women, women without any children, and women with only female children have very little say in decision-making in their marital or natal home in north-west and north-central India. Even in the matrilineal communities of South India, the brothers of the women have more decision-making powers in the household (in relation to land and other matters) than the women themselves.

Implications for poverty

Women's participation in household decision-making processes is both a value by itself and instrumental to further intra-household allocation of resources in keeping with the well-being of the family members. Less wasteful expenditure is likely as women are responsible for preparing food, caring for the sick and taking care of the household. The lesser prevalence of gender biases with respect to food, health and education in South-East Asia when compared to South Asia has been attributed to the greater decision-making power of women in the households. But this would be too simplistic to assume a direct correlation in South Asia. How far South Asian women's participation in household decision-making leads to gender-specific gains for themselves and their girl children would depend also on the extent to which they have internalised patriarchal norms in society. Though feminists claim that gender biases are higher among the men than women in the family, hard evidence is yet to be provided.

Gender-based access to Food, Health, Education and Child Care

Gender-based access pattern: a profile

Intra-household inequalities in access to resources such as food, nutrition, health and education expenditure are marked in South Asia where there is a distinct male child preference. The extent of inequality nevertheless varies in this sub-region with age, contribution to family income and labour, marital status, fertility pattern, physical ability, marriage and kinship patterns, ethnicity, and other variables (Dube, 1997, Krishnaraj *et al*, 1998). Elderly women in poor families, women who are not contributing income or productive labour to the family, widows, disabled women and women with no children or only female children tend to have lesser access to food.

In communities where marriage takes place among close relatives, such inequalities are lower than in communities where marriage takes place with distant parties. Inequalities tend to be lower or absent in matrilineal communities than in patrilineal ones. Discrimination with regard to food and access to health care persists even in higher income households, though basic nutritional needs of women and girl children may be met. Inequalities have been observed to be higher in regions where crops which are less female-intensive are grown (e.g., wheat) and lesser in regions where crops which are more female-intensive are grown (for e.g., rice) (Dyson and Moore, 1983).

The gender-based discrimination regarding access to food is less noted in most of the South-East Asian and East Asian countries. However, there is a distinct discrimination where access to education is concerned. This bias gets enhanced in periods of economic transition and crisis. In China, East Asia, there is a male child preference which is especially marked with regard to access to education. Of the 2 million children who are not in school, 70 per cent are girls (Watkins, 1998). In Vietnam, a combination of male child preference and higher demand for girl's labour in agriculture, factories and services, place girls in a disadvantaged position with regard to education. Vietnamese girls tend to enter schools at a later age, and leave earlier to help their parents generate additional income. With economic pressures increasing during the post-reform period, enrolment of girls in secondary school, distinct decreased between 1986-1987 and 1991-1992.[10]

In the PDR of Laos, though a male child preference as such is not obvious, cultural perceptions tend to place higher value on the education of boys than girls. In Indonesia and Cambodia, gender gaps in literacy and education persist, but the exact reasons could not be discerned. In Mongolia, economic considerations place boys rather than girls at a disadvantage with regard to education – i.e., the demand for male child labour is more than the demand for female child labour. This male disadvantage may in fact increase in herding families with privatisation of livestock rearing. The Philippines is another exception. Female enrolment is higher than male enrolment in schools; again the reasons are not too clear (World Bank, 1995f,g). Thus, the extent of cultural preference for sons and calculations of present and future economic returns determine girl children's access to education. Future economic returns are partly shaped by kinship and post-marital residence patterns in South Asia.

Gender disparities regarding access to health care have existed for a long time in South Asia (Tinker et al, 1994). In Vietnam, the PDR of Laos, Cambodia and Mongolia, the overall resources allocated to health care have come down during the process of transition. In this region there has been a marked rise in maternal mortality. In Vietnam these measures have brought back traditional hierarchies, and gender-specific differences with regard to access to health care have been noted (Asian Development Bank, 1995). Access to health care and education is also shaped by the physical proximity of services, availability of transport, the provision of services in a gender-sensitive form and the budget allocated to social services and its spatial allocation. Women and girl children in rural and remote areas are particularly disadvantaged, in communities where restrictions on mobility and division of domestic labour are marked. Women/adolescent girls are not only socially restricted from interacting with men, but the male health workers and teachers inhibit them from availing health and education services. This is especially true among women belonging to the upper castes and minorities in South Asia. Ethnic minorities are disadvantaged when teachers and health workers do not speak the local language, as in the case of Vietnam (Asian Development Bank, 1995a). In China women in poor provinces face a peculiar problem with financial decentralisation. They have lesser equitable access to health and education services, as these are located in provinces with limited capacity to raise revenue (Mukherjee, 1998, Bloom, G, and G, Xingyuan, 1997).

In the Philippines, state policies do not provide for abortion services, thereby placing women in a particularly disadvantaged position. These constraints lead to a greater reliance of women and girl children on unregistered medical practitioners, increasing their vulnerability to risks. The over-emphasis on family planning, reproductive health and AIDS in most of the Asian countries has taken attention away from addressing basic health needs of the poor women, and also of those women in the non-reproductive age. Occupational health needs of working women have also been neglected.

Not many state governments have paid attention to provide child care services for working women, or paid attention to introducing technologies to reduce women's domestic work burden. Fuel efficient stoves and biogas have been introduced in South Asia in the context of addressing deforestation, rather than women's practical needs. In many of the socialist countries/former socialist countries expenditure on child care has been dramatically reduced in the process of reform (Vietnam) or transition (CIS countries).

Impact on poverty of women

Gender disparities regarding women's access to food, education and health care have a direct bearing on the ability of women to meet their basic needs. Within poor households, gender disparities regarding access to these resources may make women and girl children poorer than their male counterparts. Even in households where productive endowments and income levels permit household members to overcome poverty, women members may actually be poor when intra-household inequalities are marked as in the case of north-western and north-central parts of India, northern Pakistan, and far western hills and mountains and the central hills of Nepal. The impact of women's access to child care on women's poverty is more indirect. Child care is a must for women with infants and toddlers to enter into the paid labour force, and earn in order to reduce their poverty and increase their bargaining power within the household. Child care is also necessary if women are to find the time to access government programmes, attend community meetings and mobilise community resources to meet their needs and that of their families.[11]

Among these different variables, perhaps women's access to or lack of access to education has a greater bearing on their poverty. Apart from the intrinsic value of education to the well-being of women and girl children, education also has an instrumental bearing on their well-being and that of their family members through reducing infant mortality, gender bias in food and education, and fertility rate. As pointed out by Sen (1996), one of the key factors to explain China and Vietnam's superior performance with regard to poverty reduction (and reduction of gender inequalities) compared to India, is their investment in elementary education and literacy, particularly in women's education and literacy. The pre-crisis experience of capitalist countries within South-East Asia and East Asia also points to the centrality of basic and even higher education (especially among women) for making use of whatever opportunities arise due to globalisation, privatisation and liberalisation. At a more micro level, Murthi, Guio and Dreze (1996) have shown the importance of female literacy (and labour force participation rates) to determine gender bias, infant mortality and fertility in India. The argument that women's access to health and child care also has both intrinsic and instrumental value to address their gender-specific needs and interests is definitely valid, but its instrumental use may be less than that of female education and literacy.

Gender and Space to Organise

The existing space for women to organise

Many countries in Asia were yet to sign in 1994 the ILO convention (No. 87) on the right of labourers to organise. Except Bangladesh and Pakistan in South Asia, Myanmar and the Philippines in South-East Asia and Mongolia in East Asia, all the other Asian countries were yet to ratify the Convention. On the other hand, most of the countries of the CIS had signed the Convention, other than Armenia and Moldova (World Bank, 1995a).

In authoritarian regimes like South Korea, China, Myanmar and Indonesia, the space for women to organise around their practical needs and strategic interests is less. This is also true of Islamic regimes like Pakistan and Bangladesh during the period of Ershad. In China and Indonesia the women's movement is closely identified with women's organisations which have either been formed by the state, or function with its approval. The space for autonomous groups to organise is limited. For example, the All China Women's Federation – the largest women's organisation is affiliated to the Chinese Party. In Indonesia, the government has organised wives of government officials into the Women's Welfare Movement, KOWANI and BKOW at the national, provincial and district level respectively with which it functions closely. Amongst the CIS countries, the space to organise has increased with the process of transition, but it is not clear whether there are any sub-regional variations in this respect. The women's movement is comparatively stronger in the Philippines and India, where women participated in great numbers in the nationalist movements. However, even here it tends to be led by middle class women. Across much of Asia, it is only in the late 1980s that the women's movement started to recognise the differences amongst women on the basis of religious, ethnic, class and sexual identities (Basu, 1997, Howell, 1995, World Bank, 1995c). At the regional and sub-regional level, the space to organise does exist, though constrained by inter-country dynamics. A tentative indication of the presence or absence of regional/sub-regional groups across different issues related to poverty and human rights is provided in Chapter 5.

Impact on poverty

The availability of space to organise has a more indirect bearing on poverty of women from marginalised sections. It affects their ability to:
- Organise and overcome dis-economies of small scale production.
- Unionise and demand rights to land and higher wages.
- Address corrupt practices of government which deny them access to health, education and other programmes.
- Bargain within the household for a greater share of the resources and greater male responsibility.

Thus the space to organise can help them overcome, or reduce the effect of the problems posed by the other determinants of poverty.

Gender Differentiated Impact of Key Developments in the Regions

Some of the key developments of the last two decades include:
- Globalisation and flow of trade, capital, technology and culture.[12]
- Rise in environmental degradation (partly a result of the former).
- Collapse of the communist block in USSR.

- Increase in nuclearisation especially in South Asia and China.
- Rise in religious fundamentalism in parts of South Asia and the Moslem countries of the CIS, and ethnic conflicts in different parts of Asia.[13]

Let us now concentrate on examining how the gender-based differences in resources and responsibilities mediate the impact of globalisation, and environmental degradation, as these trends are likely to affect most of Asia and the CIS. Of particular concern is their implication on women and poverty.[14] However, we also have to consider other aspects which have had their impact like:

The collapse of the Communist Block in the USSR has had a direct impact on the lives of women in the former USSR republics, as well as socialist countries in Asia. As mentioned in different parts of the report, the gender-specific implications for women in the CIS include loss of jobs, loss of social security (especially for single women), loss of rights to land and to political participation. Culturally, patriarchal values, kept down in the socialist era, have been noted to resurface in Muslim countries, leading to the re-emergence of the practice of dowry and early marriage. In non-Muslim countries like Ukraine, the socio-cultural problems may be slightly different.

Family support systems are dwindling, and recently, cases where single women are turning to prostitution have been observed. The collapse of the Communist Block has also had a bearing on women's lives in socialist countries in Asia. In Vietnam a large number of (state-run) cooperative enterprises exporting handicrafts and other goods to the former Communist Blocks have closed down. As a result, the workers – predominantly women – have lost their jobs and turned to farming or started working in the informal sector under unstable and unsafe conditions, with low pay and long working hours. At the same time, a series of private run handicraft enterprises have emerged, mainly run by women from better off sections with the objective of generating profits and employment for family members.

The rise in fundamentalism in South and Central Asia has led to the strengthening of deep-rooted patriarchal values, especially related to the institutions of family, motherhood and religion. This may have an adverse impact on women's rights to resources, mobility, public decision-making processes, and ultimately on their poverty. In Afghanistan, the Taliban has in fact banned girls from attending educational institutions, which could lead to further deterioration in literacy levels. Historically, communal battles have been fought on the battlefield on the bodies of men, and outside over the bodies and lives of women. But while peace negotiations reduce wars on the battlefield, those outside continue. As aptly put by Sen (1998:12), 'Fundamentalism is particularly problematic as it breeds on the marginalisation and loss of control amongst young men, and often encompasses a critique of globalisation even as it intensifies the subordination of women to patriarchal control.'

The rise in nuclearisation and conflicts is likely to increase expenditure on defence even further than the present high levels in India and Pakistan, and may reduce resources available for basic needs. Women are likely to bear the brunt of reduction in social service expenditure. In the areas where nuclear tests are conducted, the health of women and girl children may be affected in sex-specific ways. Women are particularly prone to reproductive health problems. Problems related to pregnancy have led to high levels of maternal mortality. At the same time, women may have lesser means to get themselves treated. Though economic sanctions have been imposed on both Pakistan and India by some of the western countries, they may affect Pakistan more than India. Trade and regional cooperation within South Asia may also be affected as a result of the conflict.

Impact of Globalisation on Women in Asia and the CIS

Different sub-regions and countries in Asia and the CIS are integrated with the global economy to different extents. There are two broad approaches to measuring the extent of integration: evaluation of the barriers to integration and evaluation of the outcome of integration. Average tariffs, non-tariff barrier coverage ratios, and indicators of capital controls are all useful indicators for evaluating the barriers to integration. Tariffs were highest in India (30 per cent), followed by China, the Philippines and Sri Lanka (all over 20 per cent), and were the least in Malaysia (9.1 per cent), followed by Ukraine (all less than or equal to 10 per cent). Of the nine countries[15] on which data on the mean average tariff was available, none had removed all tariff barriers to integration (World Bank, 1998). This may be equally true of the other countries in Asia and the CIS as well.

Two key outcome measures of integration into the global economy include the ratio of trade to GDP (which measures product market integration) and gross-capital flows to GDP (which measures capital market integration). Both are measured in international dollars using purchasing power conversion factors.

Impact of Trade on Women's Employment

Data across 27 Asian/CIS countries reveal that the extent of contribution of trade to GDP varies from 4.3 per cent in Nepal to 316.0 per cent in the case of Singapore. In general, the South Asian countries are less integrated than the South-East Asian or East Asian countries, with the exception of Sri Lanka. Within South-East Asia, the capitalist countries may be more integrated into the global economic system than the Maekhong belt, though the degree of contribution of trade to GDP in the latter region is higher than the average for South Asia. East Asia reveals a mixed picture. The Republic of Korea is perhaps more integrated than most of the South-East Asian countries, but in the case of China the contribution of trade to GDP is closer to the South Asian average.[16] The contribution of trade to GDP in the case of the countries of the CIS ranges from 9 to 41 per cent, making it difficult to generalise about the extent of integration. Amongst the CIS countries Moldova is most dependent on trade, and Georgia the least.[17]

At a theoretical level, an increase in the importance of trade in an economy is likely to influence the distribution of jobs between tradeable and non-tradeable production sectors, and hence bring more women into the paid productive labour force. Further, given the fact that women's labour is cheaper than men's labour, an increase in reliance of labour-intensive export-oriented growth is likely, with all other things remaining the same and leading to more paid employment opportunities for women than men. Women's (social) tendency to be more docile than men may also make them more attractive to employers. Trade, in theory, should also lead to rise in real wages in developing countries and improved income distribution (Joekes and Weston, 1994). Joekes and Weston's empirical analysis of the link between changes in past trade flows and the pattern of women's economic activities in developing countries (including Sri Lanka, capitalist South-East Asia and East Asia) overall, supports this theory,[18] subject to certain major qualifications:

i) **The link between expansion in trade and increase in paid female employment is stronger in the manufacturing and service sector, than in the agriculture sector.** Given that women workers in South Asia, China in East Asia, Cambodia, the PDR of Laos, Vietnam, Indonesia, Thailand and Myanmar in South-East Asia and Tajikistan in the CIS are more engaged in agriculture than in industry or services, they are less likely to benefit in terms of employment from trade. These, unfortunately, are the countries ranking low or medium in terms of human/gender development.

The reasons for women accruing less employment benefits from agricultural trade are several. Gender-based restrictions on women's independent access to land, credit, extension services and markets, as well as the division of responsibilities between subsistence and cash crop cultivation – all have a bearing on women's employment gains from agricultural trade. In the Philippines, where cultivation of cash crops is considered the domain of men, and subsistence crop the domain of women, the expansion of production of cash crops for export eroded women's role in agriculture. In the case of small peasant farmers who have shifted entirely to cash crop production, the woman's role has changed from an independent manager of subsistence production to working as unpaid labourer in her husband's farms. Wherever small farming families have chosen to combine subsistence and cash crop production, women's work burden has increased substantially, without any increase in their access to paid employment, cash income or other benefits.

A third category of small farming families in the Philippines has sold off their lands, turning both women and men into agricultural labourers or migrant unskilled labourers. While some of them have benefitted from the expansion of employment in agro-business, such employment has been highly seasonal and the quantum of work has depended on yields. On the whole, the impact of trade on Filipino women involved in agriculture may be negative (Oliveros, 1997).

ii) **Even in the manufacturing sector, the extent to which women's employment increases relative to that of men with the expansion of trade, depends to a significant extent on norms on the gender-based division of labour, investment in female literacy and education by national governments, gender-related norms on mobility, the age group and marital status of the women concerned, and the technology/production process adopted.**

Export industries in Asia have in the past created more female employment per dollar invested than domestic industries. Most of the export industries are involved in production of clothing, toys, sporting goods, electrical goods assembly, food-processing, and jewellery which are relatively more female labour-intensive, when compared to domestic parts of industry involved in heavy industry and chemical processing. Research on EPZs has surpassed research on other kinds of export-oriented manufacturing units.[19] These studies reveal that employment in these zones expanded very rapidly in the 1980s, though their significance varies with the size of the country and the stage of industrial advancement. According to one estimate, four million workers were employed in EPZs in developing countries, of whom 70 per cent were women. While EPZs are indeed female labour-intensive, the benefits have not reached evenly across sub-regions or countries in Asia.[20]

Excluding China,[21] nine countries (including Malaysia and Sri Lanka) provided three quarters of all employment in EPZs in developing countries. Women in South-East Asia and Sri Lanka have had greater access to employment in EPZs than women from other South Asian countries, due to higher levels of female literacy and skills, and more liberal gender-related norms on mobility and interaction with men. But even here they are found more in the bottom rungs of the workforce, than as supervisors who are predominantly men. Young unmarried women with some level of schooling have had greater access to employment in EPZs than older, illiterate, married women with children, as the employers prefer to keep labour costs low. This trend is however reducing in some countries like the Republic of Korea, wherein married women are finding employment in EPZs.

Changes in production processes have in some places led to a shift from factory-based production system (like the EPZs) to sub-contracting of work to home-based production units and units comprising of small worksheds. While on the one hand this has increased married women's access to employment further as they can more easily combine it with housework, it has pushed them further into the unregulated informal sector. It has also decreased the space for women to come out of their homes and gather as a collective. The implications of the move from the 'Fordist production process' (which demands skills in one specific aspect of production, and hence relatively easier to acquire) towards 'just in time production' process (demanding highly skilled workforce, familiar with different stages of the production) on women has been little researched. Once again, women's lesser access to education and training may place them in a disadvantaged position, while on the other hand the greater reliance on sub-contracting in the 'just in time production' process may be advantageous to women. In the case of Singapore, there has not been so much an increase in subcontracting as shift to more capital and high technology-intensive productive processes, leading to loss of female employment.

iii) **The extent to which women's strategic gender interests has been addressed with increase in industrial export varies.** Again studies are more abundant on the impact of employment on women in EPZs than industrial exorts in Geneva. On the negative side, several studies in SE Asia and Sri Lanka have shown how women workers in EPZs work under extremely exploitative conditions. According to these studies, women are faced with long working hours, and their work fetches low remuneration. When compared to that of men, women have insecure working conditions – they lack access to maternity leave and lack rights to organise. Sexual harassment and the dingy living conditions have also been noted. On the other hand, others have observed that women in EPZs fare better than in domestic industries, even if conditions are poor compared to those available for men in the same country or for women in developed countries. In the context of South Asia, it has offered women a space to get away from patriarchal rules dictated by their families and communities, and exercise some degree of freedom (Banerjee, 1977). As argued by Joekes and Weston (1994), the real picture may be more complicated, and it may be possible to reconcile these different points of view. They argue that in its early stages, EPZs generally offer wages which are higher than other local industries, but with time, the wages more or less equalise.

Gender-based discrimination in wages tend to be higher among married workers than among young, single persons. The insecurity in working conditions may also vary across countries. Women employed in older sites in the Philippines, for example, are losing their employment to women in new lower wage sites like in Bangladesh. On the whole, the employment opportunities and wage benefits for women in EPZs are essentially of short-term nature, associated with the early phases of a developing country's export competitiveness in light assembly and low-technology manufactures.

iv) **Even the gains for women from expansion of trade in services may be uneven and short-lived (Heeks, 1998).** Service industries tend to be labour- and more female labour-intensive than both agriculture and manufacturing. New activities such as offshore data processing, invoicing, office administration, software development and financial services are being established and are expanding in Asian countries such as China, the Philippines and Singapore. Like light manufacturing industries, these service export-oriented industries rely heavily on female labour. However, they demand higher education levels than jobs in light industries. Further, even jobs in the export-oriented service sector may prove to be short-lived with technological advancement. The emergence of technology like the 'scanner' which automatically transfers printed material into computer language is replacing women engaged in word-processing.

v) **Even if new export capacity in manufacturing and services open up job opportunities for women, one also needs to consider what activities may be eliminated and what jobs may be displaced as a result of integration into the global economy.** Women in some of the traditional handicraft industries in India have lost out as a result of the flood of handicraft items from other countries, though exact estimates are not available. In the Philippines, the closures and retrenchments caused by the World Trade Organization (WTO) implementation affected 21,830 workers in 1995, of whom women constituted a significant majority. When the present system of quotas in export of garments under the Multi-Fibre Agreements is phased out, the employment opportunities for women may decline as exports of garments decline with increase in competition (WIDE, 1996). In Kyrgyzstan several state-owned enterprises closed down when faced with competition from multinationals (MNCs) and private enterprises. The first to be fired or sent on compulsory vacations without pay were women. Unemployment rates among women are as high as 70 to 80 per cent. The state-owned enterprises which seemed viable were turned over to private owners.

However, production was hampered by difficulties encountered to access raw materials, the underdeveloped tax system, low financial position of consumers and lack of possible avenues for exports. In particular, the closing down of trade openings among the former republics which were earlier part of the Union of Soviet Socialist Republics (USSR), posed a major problem. Though some of the women who were retrenched started using traditional skills in embroidery to produce cushions and rugs for commercial purposes, the employment generated was irregular and not governed by any legal regulation. Some women are turning to pornography and prostitution to ensure their own survival and that of their families, while others are marrying off their daughters young, sometimes even at the age of fourteen (Network of East West Women, 1996, 1998a, b).

vi) **Any analysis of product market integration on women's work has to take into account that in the recent past such expansion has been embedded in most developing countries in the context of structural adjustment policies. Also, the consequences of some of these have not been positive for women.** Efforts to rationalise the bureaucracy and privatise non-viable state enterprises have displaced women workers and pushed them to work under more exploitative conditions in the informal sector. Is this displacement, along with that through trade, lesser than the employment created for women through expansion of trade? Is the feminisation of the workforce in the export-oriented industries and service sector in some of the countries an outcome of increase in levels of impoverishment – a consequence of adjustment – or is it an exercise of informed choice on the part of women? Apart from forcing some women into paid employment, structural adjustment policies may have also increased the overall work burden of women. Cuts in government spending on social services like health, education, child care, care of the elderly and supply of coal in some countries have increased women's work burden. Cuts in subsidies in education in some of the Asian countries has had gender-differentiated impact, especially when socio-cultural norms promote the education of boys over girls. In Vietnam, cut in subsidies for the education sector have led to a greater increase in dropouts of girls than boys (Do Thi Binh and Le Ngoc, 1997). This has also been observed in the case of Kyrgyzstan, where hierarchical gender norms which prevailed during the pre-socialist era have resurfaced. Educational disadvantage may have a long-term detrimental impact on women's ability to make use of employment created through industrialisation and modernisation (Harwin and Fajth, 1998).

vii) **Expansion of trade may not change women's distribution of time between paid and unpaid work as much as enhance women's total workload.** Expansion of women's engagement in paid employment has not been accompanied by any significant change in the gender-based division of responsibilities with regard to domestic work, child care and the care of the elderly. As a result, women's overall work burden may have increased with expansion of trade, especially in instances where women have entered the labour market for the first time (Elson, 1991).

Impact of Free-Trade on Women's Access to Food and Seeds

Given that the possibilities of expanding land under cultivation have been exhausted in most Asian countries, expansion of trade has in fact reduced land under cultivation. Growth in trade in industrial goods and services has been higher than growth in trade in agriculture. Combined with the rapid increase in urbanisation[22] and expansion of infrastructure[23] in Asia, it is not uncommon to find land being diverted for non-farm use.[24] Further, there has been a decrease in proportion of land being used for cultivation of food grains, as non-food cash crops are more profitable to export. At the same time, grain productivity is declining due to environmental degradation and saturation of gains from the use of fertilisers. Free-trade also affects the allocation of grains between human and animal consumption. The substantial demand for animal feed in the developed countries is leading to the diversion of a small, but significant proportion of food grains for this purpose. According to Gardner (1997), this combination of trends may soon threaten the food security of Asian countries in particular (Braun J V, 1995, FAO, 1995, Suryanarayana, 1997).

Another point of concern is that the terms of trade have not really improved in favour of agriculture with liberalisation of trade, as was predicted by the World Bank. European governments are yet to dismantle subsidies for their farmers, hence producers in the developing countries continue to be disadvantaged (Mies, 1996). Restrictions on market access for exporting agricultural products into the developed countries continue in spite of liberalisation. Similarly, the practice of fixing floor prices for food grain procurement (often below the market rate) by national governments has as yet not been dismantled in South Asia. On the whole, the terms of trade have not really improved in favour of agriculture, or led to an increase in food production (World Bank, 1998). In the case of the CIS countries, the sudden lack of preferential access to the former USSR market with freeing up of trade led to lowered agriculture production in the region (Brown, 1997, Gardner, 1997).

Any future improvement in terms of trade in favour of agriculture (with the total opening up of agricultural trade) is likely to have a different impact on food importing and exporting countries. Several

Asian countries have either already crossed the import dependency threshold[25] or are likely to cross this threshold by the year 2020. The list includes Sri Lanka, Afghanistan, Bangladesh, and Pakistan in South Asia, Republic of Korea, Democratic People's Republic of Korea and China in East Asia, and Malaysia, Indonesia, the Philippines in South-East Asia (Gardner, 1997). Though data on the CIS countries falling below the import threshold were not available, food production is likely to fall drastically in Kazakhstan (now a net importer of wheat) due to soil erosion. People in these countries may face a rise in food prices with total dismantling of barriersto free trade in agriculture. Landless labourers and marginal farmers in rural areas, and the urban poor may be affected to a greater extent than the big farmers as they are dependent on purchase of food in the open market. In South Asia, women and girl children among this group may be more affected than their male counterparts as intra-household gender inequalities persist in the distribution of food.

In the case of those countries which are likely to be net exporters of food grains, the benefits of increase in food prices may not accrue evenly. Big farmers with access to credit, inputs, and extension services may benefit more than small and marginal farmers.

Women farmers in food exporting countries may reap fewer benefits than men as they have little access to credit, inputs and extension services, and in South Asia also to land. The evidence of women's loss of rights to land in Vietnam and Cambodia with de-collectivisation may have adverse consequences on their ability to make use of any improvements in terms of trade in favour of agriculture in the future. Further, women farmers' control over the produce is greater in the case of subsistence crops, than cash crops. Shifts towards the latter may reduce the food security of women and their families. Any improvement in terms of trade is also likely to have an adverse impact on the urban poor and the rural landless labourers in these countries, especially when combined with the removal of consumer subsidies. Among these groups women may be more affected than men in South Asia, given the intra-household inequalities in the distribution of food.

The earlier possibility of increasing food security in Asia by expanding the catch of fish – a cheap source of animal protein – has also declined in the 1990s, with stagnation in growth in this sector. In particular, the growth in fish catch per person in South-East Asian coastal areas has come to a halt in the 1990s as a result of these processes. With the reforms commencing in the 1990s in South Asia, a similar process of marginalisation has set in the coastal zones of this sub-region. In China, recording the world's highest fish catch, artisanal fishworkers have been marginalised though the coastal areas have prospered (Brown, 1997). Again a substantial proportion of the Asian catch of fish is being diverted for production of animal feed.

The recent experience in India wherein an attempt was made to patent the products of the neem tree portends the dangers of things to come with the introduction of Trade Related Intellectual Property Rights (TRIPS). Communities have used neem for thousands of years as pesticides, disinfectants and for general good health. Women, in particular, are repositories of this knowledge. When Larson, an American from the USA, acquired the patent for all Neem products and sold it to the mulitnational W R Grace, he had not discovered anything new, but had made the ancient Indian knowledge his private property and then sold it. This meant that Indians who wish to produce anything from neem have to pay license fees to Larsen and W R Grace. Fortunately, activists fought successfully against this bio-piracy before the US patent office (Mies, 1996). A struggle is also going on against the patenting and introduction of terminator seeds by MNCs in India.

Impact of Freeing Capital Markets on Women

Apart from trade, another indicator of globalisation is the contribution of gross capital flows – the sum of the absolute values of direct, portfolio and other investment inflows and outflows recorded in the balance of payments – in percentage to GDP.[26] An analysis of this figure for 21 countries reveals that the capital markets in South Asian countries (with the exception of Sri Lanka) are integrated to a much lesser extent when compared to capitalist countries in South-East Asia or East Asia. Data on the CIS reveals a mixed picture. The contribution of gross capital flows to GDP ranges from 11.6 per cent in the case of the Russian Federation (almost the figure for Republic of Korea) to 2.9 per cent in the case of Armenia (slightly above the South Asia average).

Proponents of capital – market integration argue that the free flow of capital into developing countries can increase investment and fuel growth. While the South-East Asian/East Asian case supports this hypothesis, it also reveals that these countries become extremely vulnerable to sudden movements in capital. The recent South-East Asian/East Asian crisis also portends what could happen in the coming future when financial sector reforms do not precede opening up of financial markets, and when factors beyond a country's control take over (Rao, 1998, DAWN-SE Asia, 1998, Commins et al, 1998, World Bank, 1998, Robb, 1998, Stewart, 1998, CIROAP, 1998).[27]

Illustrating the possible implications of freeing capital flows on the poor/women using Thailand as a case study, wherein the crisis manifested itself first: By the end of 1997, an estimated one to 2.9 million people lost jobs. The first affected were factory workers, construction, taxi sdrivers and casual workers in urban areas, who were laid off due to the closure of industries, slowing down of construction of buildings, and general recession in the economy. Exact estimates on how much proportion of this group are women could not be gathered, but a majority of the factory workers according to the Forum for Women in Thailand, were women.

Many of those affected have started migrating back to the villages from which they hailed, i.e., predominantly from North-Eastern Thailand. As the labour absorptive power of the agriculture sector itself is low, indirect ripples can be seen in this belt wherein poverty levels have been noted to increase. Others have opted to stay back, but send less or no remittances to their elderly family members left behind, a large proportion of whom are women. Some have also noted the tendency of circular migration – from Bangkok to rural areas/small towns and back to Bangkok – in search of jobs. Irrespective of their location, people in Thailand are faced with rising food prices (which unfortunately have not benefitted farmers).[28] Interest rates have soared high, and access to credit is a major issue. Budget cuts in health and education as a result of the IMF and World Bank conditionalities, along with the bail out package, have added to the problems of both urban and rural women in Thailand, pushing them to increase the number of hours of their work.

Children's education has been affected as some of them have been forced to pull their children out of school for employment opportunities. Gender bias has been noted by some. Handicapped children – both girls and boys – from poor families have been pushed into begging as a survival strategy. Women and girls have been affected in certain gender specific ways as well. Some in the North-East have been pushed into the sex trade to bail out their families, and this trend may increase. Other groups affected are migrant domestic and workers from Burma, Indonesia and Cambodia in Thailand as well as unskilled workers from Thailand in Malaysia, who are being sent back. Incidence of conflicts is also noted to have increased during the last year.

Impact of Globalisation of Technology on Women

Some of the changes in international trade and finance reflect advances in technology – in particular, communication technologies. Further, to be competitive in the global markets, adoption of the latest production technologies is a must. Proponents of globalisation argue that it should lead to a freer flow of technologies across countries (but with higher costs through patenting), and increased productivity of labour leading to rise in wages (UNDP, 1997). However, technology is neither scale, nor gender neutral (Ahmed, I, 1985).

Poor women's lesser access to land, capital, credit, extension services, training and education may imply that they have lesser access than their male counterparts and women from privileged groups to new useful technologies which emerge. For example, computer aided design and quality control systems have by-passed poor women's groups involved in garment exports in South Asia, making them less competitive.

Further, not all production technologies may be beneficial for women. Some in fact may displace workers in general, and women workers in particular.[29] In the last two decades, agricultural technology has displaced women workers, and this trend may increase with globalisation. In Indonesia, paddy was traditionally harvested by women using the *ani-ani* (single blade implement), and women were paid a share of the total harvest, in kind. The introduction of labour saving sickles, more suited to new high yielding short straw rice varieties, has displaced female labour. The shift from the *bawon* system of universal participation in harvesting operations, to a closed *ceblokon* system wherein payments are made in cash, and male labourers are preferred, has been detrimental for poor women.

The introduction of the rice hulling equipment has also drastically reduced women wage labourers work opportunities, while providing relief to upper class women (World Bank, 1996e). Similar displacement of landless women was noted in Bangladesh and India with the introduction of rice mills, and in the Philippines when harvesting technology similar to Indonesia was introduced. In the sugar industry, mechanisation released at least 35 per cent of women workers in the Philippines. In the fisheries sector, fisherwomen in much of Asia (especially South-East Asia) lost out due to mechanisation of fishing. Motorised *bancas* introduced recently have increased the catch of fish, and now men convey the catch directly to wholesale fish markets (ICSF, 1997, World Bank, 1995g, 1996j).

In the service sector, technologies like the scanner have started replacing women involved in word processing.

Another point of concern is the misuse of genetic engineering and biotechnology, which in conjunction with patenting of seeds could lead to the dominance of terminator seeds in developing countries. This would increase the dependency of farmers on outsiders for procurement of seeds, increase costs of inputs and reduce bio-diversity. As women are repositories of knowledge on seed production, the misuse of biotechnology could also see a decline in the role of women in seed production and in agriculture (Shiva, 1996).

In fisheries, the growth of commercial acquaculture in Asia (particularly in China and India)[30] has led to the depletion of fisheries resources and the salination of land and drinking water (ICSF, 1997). In the Philippines, the growth of aquaculture has led to the displacement of women crab collectors. Consequently, women crab collectors have migrated from the Philippines to other countries as domestic workers. In the processing sector, the introduction of ice storage systems has displaced women involved in fish processing in many Asian countries. There is also a serious threat to traditional processing technology used by women.

Impact of Globalisation of Culture on Women

The globalisation of the economy has been aided and accompanied by globalisation of the media. Western consumerist styles have to be promoted to accommodate increase in production and consumption of goods.

To reduce their domestic workload and influenced by the different advertisements through global channels, middle and upper class women in Asia, like their western counterparts, have started adopting various technologies. These range from washing machines and grinders, to instant foods. Some of the Asian upper and middle class women, influenced by role models from a slightly more liberated western culture, have also started challenging gender hierarchies. The more visible needs are being redefined with the spread of this global culture, leading to lower priority being placed on consumption of nutritious food. As needs increase at a rate faster than income, poor women may be forced to reduce their consumption of goods essential for survival.

The rise in consumerism has also led to increase in traditional forms of violence against women. In South Asia the practice and quantum of dowry have increased. This practice has spread to previously non-practising groups like the labouring class, dalits and tribals. In fact, this is the main route for men from these groups to acquire consumer goods which they see in the market. In South-East Asia, not only poor women, but also those from middle and upper classes are turning to prostitution so as to afford a western lifestyle.

On the whole, globalisation portends little room for optimism for poor women in Asia and the CIS. On the one hand, it may increase their access to employment, but on the other, it may not enhance their control over labour or their access to an often neglected basic need – rest. Women belonging to groups identified earlier – landless labourers, marginal and small farmers, fisherfolk, women dispossessed of land and bonded labourers are going to be more affected than those belonging to the privileged groups.

In this context, one of the key concerns is the absence of a separate Committee on Gender and Trade within the WTO, ASEAN, APEC, SAARC and other regional organisations, with a charter to promote gender equitable standards in international trade; and at the same time ensure that the clause is not used against the interest of developing countries. As of 1997 a committee on Environment and Trade does exist within WTO due to the strong lobbying power of the environmental movement. There is also a need to follow up on the recommendation at the Social Summit that a Tobin Tax on trade be adopted, and ensure that funds raised are used in the interest of poor women and men in developing countries.

Impact of Environmental Degradation and Disasters on Women

Environmental degradation has had a longer history when compared to the rapid globalisation of economies in the 1990s. While environmental degradation may increase in the 1990s with expansion of trade,[31] the impact of this phenomenon on women in Asia and the CIS may need to be looked at independently.

Economic growth in South-East Asia and South Asia from 1981–95 seems to have been accompanied by deforestation, unlike East Asia and the CIS countries where the rate of deforestation has been fairly low during this period. In most of the CIS countries, aforestation rather than deforestation seems to have taken place. However, there are marked inter-country and intra-country variations in the rate of deforestation in South Asia and South-East Asia. In South Asia the rate of deforestation was higher in Pakistan and Bangladesh during the period 1981–90, and lower in India and Bhutan during this period. In South-East Asia, the rate of deforestation was higher in the Philippines, Thailand and Malaysia during both the periods, and lower in Indonesia and the Maekhong belt. Though on the whole Mongolia records little deforestation, there are pockets in which rates of deforestation have been high (ADB, 1997). Deforestation in most sub-regions has been due to felling of wood for commercial interests, a significant proportion of which has been caused by multinationals in Malaysia and Indonesia (Women's Feature Service, 1992).

The impact of deforestation on women and men varies across regions, depending on the norms governing gender-based division of roles, rights and responsibilities, as well as norms governing the mobility of women and men (Ahmed, 1998). The erosion of sound ecological principles of traditional communities in Mongolia and the PDR of Laos has led to indiscriminate deforestation. Women in particular have been affected, as they bear the burden of gathering fuelwood and fetching water (ADB, 1995, World Bank, 1996). Highland women in the PDR of Laos depend heavily on the forests for food and medicinal plants, and as a result their health and nutrition levels have declined. On the other hand, in Hunza and Nagar in Northern Pakistan where rates of deforestation have been high, the rigid norms against women travelling too far away from the settlement have led to men taking over this responsibility, and it is the men whose work burden has increased (Joekes, 1989). However, in the case of elderly women living on their own, their work burden has definitely increased.

Apart from deforestation, another issue is the emergence of large infrastructure projects along rivers and coastal lines, and globalisation, commercialisation and mechanisation of the fishing sector. Large hydroelectric dam projects which have proliferated along the Mekong River in South-East Asia, are examples. (ACTIONAID-Hanoi, 1998). While these offer a source of energy for some, they have also led to riverbank erosion, siltation, flooding, and destruction of fisheries and loss of nutrients for downstream agriculture. Displaced people have not been adequately compensated where dams have been built, and the compensation money has often been directed at men, even in instances like in parts of Malaysia and Sri Lanka where women had equal rights to land (Women's Feature Service, 1992).[32]

In coastal zones of South Asia, aquaculture industries have proliferated, and resulted in salination of land, land degradation, salination/siltation of groundwater and decline in the catch of fish. Poor women's livelihoods have in particular been eroded, as fish vending is an important source of income for them. Decline in food security, nutrition (fish is an important source of nutrition) and quality of drinking water are three other concerns of women in such contexts. In the Philippines, over fishing, destructive fishing techniques and tenure licensing to aquaculture have led to conflict between locally-based artisan fishers and large commercial fishers. Fisherwomen are losing access to gleaning areas, and are being displaced (OXFAM, 1997).

Table 3.2 Deforestation across Regions 1980–95

Country	Annual rate of deforestation* (1981–90)	Annual deforestation Square kilometer	Average per cent change 1990–95
CIS Armenia	NI	-84	-2.7
Azerbaijan	NI	0	0.0
Belarus	NI	-688	-1.0
Georgia	NI	0	0.0
Kazakhstan	NI	-1,928	-1.9
Kyrgyzstan	NI	0	0.0
Moldova	NI	0	0.0
Russian Federation	NI	0	0.0
Tajikistan	NI	0	0.0
Turkmenistan	NI	0	0.0
Ukraine	NI	-54	-0.1
Uzbekistan	NI	-2,260	-2.7
Afghanistan	NI	NI	NI
East Asia China	0.4	866	0.1
Hong Kong, China Korea-D	NI NI	NI 0	NI 0.0
Korea-R	NI	130	0.2
Mongolia	NI	0	0.0
South Asia Bangladesh	3.3	88	0.8
Bhutan	0.6	NI	NI
India	0.6	-72	0.0
Maldives	NI	NI	NI
Nepal	1.7	548	1.1

Pakistan	2.9	550	2.9
Sri Lanka	1.3	202	1.1
South-East Asia Cambodia	1.0	1,638	1.6
Indonesia	1.7	10,844	1.0
PDR of Laos	0.9	-	-
Malaysia	1.8	4,002	2.4
Myanmar	1.2	3,874	1.4
Philippines	2.9	2,624	3.5
Singapore	-	0	0.0
Thailand	2.9	3,294	2.6
Vietnam	1.4	1,352	1.4

Source: UNDP, Human Development Report, 1997, Table 24 (for data on 1981–90)
* World Bank, World Development Indicator, 1998, Table 3.1 (for data on 1990–95)

In north China as well, women are affected by endemic water shortages, pollution and contamination. Many of the Chinese industries to be privatised are heavy polluters of cities and waste energy (ibid, 1997). According to one estimate, 1,78,000 people living in China's cities will suffer premature deaths because of pollution.

The entire region is prone to severe natural disasters, which are on the rise with the degradation of the environment. It is estimated that half of the natural disasters of the world occur in Asia (ESCAP, 1995, cited in ActionAid 1998). Parts of South-East Asia, South Asia and East Asia are prone to typhoons, floods and earthquakes. Volcanic eruptions are more common in South-East Asia. Earthquakes are common in some of the CIS countries like Armenia (World Bank, 1998a). During an emergency, women tend to be left out as they prioritise their family's safety over theirs. In some cases restrictions on their mobility also come in the way, as in Bangladesh. Relief efforts often do not address gender concerns in emergency situations, like providing separate spaces for women and children in evacuation centres, locating services in convenient spaces, the provision of supplies to women for menstruation, and the timetabling of services to suit the time schedule of women (Walker, 1996)

End Notes

1. Residence of the bride in the bridegroom's place after marriage.
2. In 1990 multilateral banks allocated $5.8 billion for rural credit to developing countries yet only 5% reached rural women (UNDP, HDR, 1995).
3. In parts of North East India exceptions may be found. Women take to ploughing in this region.
4. For reasons not clear some of the figures are not totally 100%. A clarification has been sought from the World Bank, which is yet to arrive.
5. Again, the figures do not total 100%, and a clarification has been sought.
6. The growth rate has been highest in services when compared to other sectors in the Philippines, Republic of Korea, Bangladesh, China, India, Republic of Korea, Sri Lanka.
7. Though the measures include certain variables like share of women in earned income which is not related to public decision-making.
8. Other than Vietnam, the PDR of Laos, Myanmar and Cambodia on which data on GEM index was not available.
9. In India 33% seats in local self-governance institutions have been reserved for women since 1993. But women's representation cannot be equated with participation. Instances wherein the husbands participate in meetings and take decisions instead of the women have been noted. In other cases, elected women remain silent spectators, while elected men take most decisions. Dalit women, in particular, have faced tremendous opposition to exercise their authority. As recent as 15 August 1998, a dalit woman President of the Panchayat was stripped for unfolding the national flag on Independence day.
10. From 423,600 in 1986–87 to 247,000 in 1991–92 (GSO, 1993, cited in communication with Quann, ACTIONAID-Vietnam.
11. This has affected women's ability to participate in employment, or in public decision-making. This problem may be less acute in societies and communities wherein joint family system exists. In the case of displaced women and girl children – refugees, internally displaced people, migrants – many of these problems are compounded as family, community and state support systems have been disrupted.
12. Including the transition of previously centrally managed economies in China, Vietnam, Cambodia, the PDR of Laos, and Mongolia, breaking up of the former Soviet Union and transition to capitalism, and the recent South-East Asian crisis.
13. The Pakistan government in 1998 proposed a bill on Islamisation of the state, which may lead to a similar effort to make India a Hindu state.
14. Implications on human rights violations against women (irrespective of their economic status) are examined in Chapter 4.
15. The nine countries referred to are the Russian Federation, Ukraine, China, and Republic of Korea, Indonesia, Malaysia, the Philippines, India and Sri Lanka.
16. The contribution of trade to GDP depends not just on government policies, but also factors such as country size, factor endowment, geographical isolation and stage of development.

17. A comparison of the rate of growth in trade with the rate of growth in GDP across these countries also reveals a similar picture. The growth rate in trade is higher than the growth trade in GDP by only around 3% in the case of South Asia and China. The difference is higher in the case of capitalist South-East Asian countries (Indonesia is an exception) or East Asia (minus China). Thus the argument that trade is the engine of economic growth may not be valid in all the sub-regions of Asia and the CIS.

18. Their study of share of women in manufacturing labour force in 35 developing countries against changes in the export ratio over the period 1960–85 demonstrates a strong tendency for increased exports to lead to increased employment of women in manufacturing and vice versa.

19. Bulk of the research on employment in export-oriented industries has focused on EPZs (and then TNCs), which may only represent the tip of the iceberg, as many more women are employed in small enterprises, sweat shops, home based production units engaged in exports.

20. Very little information could be gathered on EPZs in the CIS countries.

21. The situation in China is anomalous, as the Special Economic Zones in China are not exactly comparable to EPZs. They employ a much larger number of people than EPZs in any other country (Joekes and Weston, 1994).

22. In South Asia the urban population is projected to increase by some 420 million people between 1995 and 2010 implying an expansion in urban areas of 21 million hectares. This would inevitably lead to large losses of crop land (Gardner, 1997).

23. Loss of land for construction of roads has been particularly high in China in East Asia, India in South Asia, and Vietnam, Indonesia, Malaysia and Thailand in South-East Asia.

24. According to the University of Missouri, some 5% of arable land in China was pulled out from production between 1987 to 1992 due to a combination of all these processes. Though China brought new land into production during same period, the net loss in land under agricultural production was a considerable 3.87 million hectares (cited in Gardner, 1997). Unfortunately, such estimates were not available for other countries.

25. That is, import more than 20% of total grain consumption.

26. Converted to international dollars using the PPP is an indicator to measure capital market integration.

27. For example, strengthening of the dollar against the yen.

28. Traders have earned the maximum.

29. It is easier for employers to introduce labour displacing technologies amongst women than men as they are less unionised.

30. Till recently, China and India alone accounted for over 65% of the world's acquaculture production (ICSF, *Women In Fisheries*, No. 4).

31. Traditionally, developed countries have been net exporters of pollution-intensive goods, while developing countries have been net importers. With the exception of developing countries (India, China) with large reserves of mineral/natural resources, most tend not to specialise in heavily polluting industries. This comparative picture may continue with the expansion of

trade as the main endowment of developing countries is their cheap labour power, and labour-intensive industries tend to be less polluting than capital-intensive ones. However, in terms of absolute levels, this may not hold well. Export-import ratio of pollution-intensive goods of low income countries including Asia has gone up between 1986 and 1995, portending that in the long run developing countries may catch up with the pollution levels of the developed countries (World Bank, 1998). Another impact of trade on environment in developing Asia (less so in CIS where economic growth is slow) could be the rise in consumption of fuel and emission of carbon dioxide with increase in use of motorised vehicles with rise in income.

32. Batang Al dam in Sarawak, Malaysia and Mahewli Irrigation Project in Sri Lanka.

Chapter Four

Human Rights Violations against Women in the Region

The analysis of the incidence of poverty in the region among women has revealed that the problem of poverty continues to be the main challenge ahead for the decade to come. However, focusing exclusively on poverty concerns of women, can take attention away from the deep-rooted discrimination which women face qua women in every aspect of their lives.

The last decade has witnessed a significant rise in human rights violations against women in Asia and the CIS (Human Rights Watch, 1998). Globalisation, privatisation and liberalisation of the economy have resulted in new forms and scales of economic and socio-cultural exploitation of women. For example, trafficking in women has become globalised, and exploitation of women's labour takes place not just in the hands of local industrialists, but also by MNCs. There is an urgent need for new institutional structures to promote and protect violations against women by global and local market organisations. Committees on Gender and Trade within the WTO, ASEAN, APEC and SAARC would go a long way to promote human rights and gender equitable standards in international trade.

As mentioned earlier, the transition of former socialist republics to market-led democratic countries in the CIS has led to the resurfacing of traditional patriarchal norms, and erosion of many of the socio-economic and political gains made by women during the socialist regimes. In the CIS countries, which have seen a rise in fundamentalism, the trend has been more marked than in others. The weakening of the State in these countries has reduced avenues for protection and promotion of human rights of women. The breaking up of the former Soviet Union also resulted in unprecedented ethnic conflicts in the region, leading to a large number of refugees and internally displaced people. Women and children who constitute a large chunk of this group were particularly affected. A similar erosion of women's human rights has been observed in China and Vietnam (though still socialist) which are shifting from a command economy to a more market-led one. Though Cambodia traditionally had a more gender-egalitarian culture, the reforms have weakened women's rights, especially to land.

On the positive side, in the World Conference on Human Rights held in Vienna in 1993, for the first time it was recognised that women's rights were 'an inalienable, integral and indivisible' part of universal human rights. Domestic violence and sexual violence against women in times of war were for the first time recognised as human rights violations.[1] A special rapporteur on Violence Against Women was appointed in 1994 and based in Sri Lanka. In 1995, at the Fourth World Conference on Women in Beijing, the protection of women's rights was recognised as being inextricably linked with improvement of women's status. Many countries which had not ratified the Convention on the Elimination of Discrimination Against Women did so subsequently. These can be seen as an achievement of the growing international women's movement.

Similarly, despite the strengths of the Committee on the Elimination of All Forms of Discrimination Against Women (CEDAW), its effectiveness to promote women's rights remain severely compromised by inadequate technical and financial resources. Not all countries have ratified the women's convention as yet. Within Asia, Afghanistan is yet to ratify the Convention despite having signed it. The Democratic People's Republic of Korea and Myanmar are yet to sign or ratify the Convention (UNDP, 1997), and human rights violations against women is noted to be high in both these countries. Among the countries falling under the CIS, Kazakhstan, Kyrgyzstan and Turkmenistan are yet to sign the Convention (UNDP, 1997). Further, many member states of the UN have not adopted and ratified the protocol of the Convention which allows women to submit complaints directly to the Committee when their domestic legal system has failed them. The compartmentalisation of women's human rights issue within the UN is another point of concern. The UN has failed to integrate women's human rights into its treaty-based and non-treaty-based bodies' system-wide work on human rights.

Some of the countries in Asia and the CIS which have ratified the Convention Against Elimination of Discrimination Against Women are yet to ratify the International Covenant on Economic, Social and Cultural Rights, 1966; International Covenant on Civil and Political Rights, 1966; and the Convention Relating to the Status of Refugees, 1951 (see Table 4.1). Others like India have placed reservations on particular Articles of the Convention with regard to compulsory registration of marriage and reform of personal laws, stating that it interferes with the rights of citizens to practise their religion. To the extent that women's rights are regulated by family, community or religion rather than personal autonomy and individual rights, women in much of the world still face enormous obstacles in their search for redress when they have suffered abuse committed in the name of custom or tradition. This furthers the scope for violation of rights of women and women refugees (UNDP, 1997).

Gap Between Commitments and Practice

In the case of the governments which have ratified the Convention, to what extent has discrimination against women been really eliminated? The evidence gathered by the Human Rights Watch shows a wide gap between government rhetoric and practice. Some of the key gender-specific/women targeted human rights violations of women in the region include:

Trafficking of women and girl children for sexual purposes

Trafficking of women for sexual purposes has a long history in Asia. During the Second World War poor Korean women sexually served Japanese soldiers in China in 'comfort homes'.[2] The Philippines soon became the centre for trafficking in Asia, and when the government took firm measures to control this practice, the base shifted to Thailand, which now is both a receiver (from Cambodia, Vietnam and Burma) and exporter of sex workers to Korea, Japan and Europe. With the increase in globalisation, liberalisation and privatisation, cross-country movement has become easier, income inequalities have increased, and the poorest are finding it all the more difficult to survive. The result is an increase in trafficking of women for sexual purposes. Abject poverty is now driving poor women from Vietnam and Cambodia into this profession, while several are also forced into it. A few upper class women have got into this trade voluntarily, not out of poverty or by force, but attracted by the glamour of earning huge amounts in a short while (compared to local standards), living in comfort, and travelling to western countries.

Often sex workers are persecuted in non-economic ways right from their entry into the profession to finally, their exit (if they wish to leave the profession). A study carried out in the brothels along the Thailand–Cambodian border revealed that some of the Cambodian girls from poor families were tricked by agents into the trade with the promise of lucrative employment (GAATW, IOM, CWDA, 1997). A few were sold off by their parents without their consent. In many cases, however, the women were aware of the trade or profession they were entering into, but were unaware of the degree of exploitation. The study also noted that such open trafficking would have been impossible without the connivance of the government functionaries working in the borders. The entire process of globalisation and economic liberalisation has made it easier for those engaged in trafficking.

Once sex workers enter the brothels, they cannot leave it till they pay off the debt to the brothel owner or the concerned agent. They may, however, be sold to another brothel owner. They also have little say in the number or kind of clients they would like to serve, and hardly have the power to enforce the rule that the clients should use condoms. Periodically they are sent for medical check ups, and if they have contracted AIDS they are asked to leave (UNAIDS, 1997). Most women continue in the profession even after paying off the debt, so that they can save some money for their families. But the extent to which they are accepted by their families when they return varies.

Within South Asia, trafficking of women for sex trade is common in Nepal,[3] Bangladesh, Pakistan and India (Fernando, 1997, Bhatta et al, 1993, National Commission for Women, 1997). Trafficking in India takes place mainly within the country, while a significant proportion of Nepali girls are found in Indian brothels. Poverty is the main reason for this (National Commission for Women, 1997, Bhatta et al, 1993, Poudel and Shreshtha, 1996). In parts of Karnataka and Maharastra (India), poverty combines with caste-based exploitation, forcing women from the dalit community into prostitution, under the guise of the devadasi system (Murthy, 1995).

In the countries of the CIS and Eastern Europe, trafficking of women has been noted to have risen dramatically in the 1990s. It is used as a survival strategy by women who have lost their jobs, have to face declining state support, and have many children. Given the proximity of these countries to European Union member States and the relaxation of visa requirements, it is becoming easier and less expensive to bring women from these countries to Western Europe than from South-East Asia (International Organisation for Migration, 1997).

A major point of concern is that across Asia, the proportion of children to total people in prostitution is on the rise (Sachs, 1995). The threat of AIDS seems to be a major factor influencing this trend (ibid, 1995). Children's advocacy groups estimate that there are about 30,000 child prostitutes in Sri Lanka, 60,000 child prostitutes in the Philippines, 4,00,000 in India and 6,00,000 in Thailand. Most of the children are girls under 16, with the exception of Sri Lanka, where boys outnumber girls.

Other forms of trafficking of women and children

Apart from trafficking of women for sexual purposes, women in the region are also traded as marriage partners, domestic workers, child-care givers, construction workers, beggars, casual industrial workers and nurses. Many of them live in slave-like conditions. A large number of Sri Lankan women, for example, work as domestic workers in the Middle East, South Korea, and Malaysia. Some of them travel illegally, while others have legal permits. The Women and Media Collective observes that apart from the economic exploitation explained earlier, some of them are sexually exploited by the employers. Further, the customs and legislation in the receiving country may be quite different from those in the country of origin, resulting in women getting punished for behaviour which would be considered as legal in their country. A Sri Lankan domestic worker was sentenced to six months imprisonment, awarded 90 lashes and subsequently deported for having an illicit relationship with a man in Middle East Asia. In 1997 there was a total of 102 deaths of Sri Lankan migrant workers in Middle Eastern Countries. The number of suicides reported amongst domestic workers is particularly high, and needs to be looked into. Another point of concern is the fact that very little security is available to the women when they return home from the Katunayake airport. This has resulted in not so uncommon cases of abduction, robbery and rape (Women in Media Collective, 1998).

An issue which received a lot of attention recently is the case of trafficking of children (girls and boys) from Bangladesh to the Middle East for use in Camel races. It is believed that the screams of children will make the camels go faster. Trafficking of Cambodian children, especially the disabled, for begging in Thailand is another way by which children are exploited.

Violation of reproductive rights of women

A crucial indicator of women's position in society is their ability to exercise their will in the matter of reproduction. Three key issues involved are their ability to define whether to have children, how many children to have, when to have and, in case they are unable to have, to determine their status in the household. Women's rights to determine these aspects seem to vary within the Asian countries, based on State policies, family and kinship norms and dictates of the market forces.

In China, the government has strongly advocated a one-child per family norm to control the population, and numerous sources report that local Chinese officials have frequently used or condoned physical, psychological and economic coercion to enforce this norm. In 1994 China further adopted the Law of the People's Republic of China on Maternal and Infant Healthcare. Essentially a Eugenics law, this legislation threatens to undermine the right of couples with a serious hereditary disease to found a family (Ramanathan, 1997). In India also coercion is common, but more often harmful hormonal and injectable contraceptives are experimented on illiterate women who are little aware of their implications (Human Rights Watch, 1998). In contrast, in Singapore the government encourages couples to have more children as the population growth rate has declined. Thus the State plays an important role to determine what choices women have vis-à-vis reproduction.

Table 4.1: Progress with Regard to Ratification of Selected International Instruments

Country	Convention on the elimination of all forms of discrimination against women, 1979	International covenant on economic, social and cultural rights, 1966	International covenant on civil and political rights, 1966	Convention on the rights of the child, 1989	Convention relating to the status of the refugees, 1951
CIS					
Armenia	*	*	*	*	*
Azerbaijan	*	*	*	*	*
Belarus	*	*	*	*	-
Georgia	*	*	*	*	-
Kazakhstan	-	-	-	*	-
Kyrgyzstan	-	*	*	*	*
Moldova	*	*	*	*	-
Russian Federation	*	*	*	*	*
Tajikistan	*	-	-	*	*
Turkmenistan	-	-	-	*	-
Ukraine	*	*	*	*	-
Uzbekistan	*	*	*	*	-
East Asia					
Hong Kong, China					
China	*	-	-	*	*

Korea-D	-	*	*	-
Korea-R	*	*	*	*
Mongolia	*	*	*	*
South Asia				
Afghanistan	-	*	*	-
Bangladesh	*	-	*	-
Bhutan	*	-	*	-
India	*	*	*	*
Maldives	*	-	*	-
Nepal	*	*	*	-
Pakistan	*	-	*	-
Sri Lanka	*	*	*	-
South-East Asia				
Cambodia	*	*	*	*
Indonesia	*	-	*	-
PDR of Laos	*	-	*	-
Malaysia	*	-	*	-
Myanmar	-	-	*	-
Philippines	*	*	*	*
Singapore	*	-	*	*
Thailand	*	*	*	-
Vietnam	*	*	*	-

Note: "*Those that have ratified." "-"indicates the non-ratification.   Source: UNDP, 1997, Table 48.

Other institutions play an important role as well. In much of South Asia, a married woman who chooses not to have a child is likely to face the opposition of her husband, marital and natal family. It is taken for granted that the woman is to blame if she does not conceive. Further, the inability to produce a child is customarily seen as a legitimate reason for the husband to go in for a second marriage, even if legally it is not permitted. Apart from the family and kinship structures and community level institutions, in recent times market-organisations have started playing an important role in shaping a woman's reproductive options. Many EPZs retrench women once they get married or become pregnant, due to the maternity benefits that they would have to provide. Questions on their reproductive behaviour are often raised during interviews by their prospective employers.

Violation of rights of female infants and foetus to live

A particular aspect of women's reproductive rights is their ability to decide to have a girl child. In parts of Tamil Nadu, Rajasthan and Bihar (India) women do not always have this right, and are forced to kill their female infants/agree for the infants to be killed. In the more prosperous parts of Western and Northern India, female foeticide is more common than infanticide (Murthy, 1997). In China also the male child preference is very marked, and incidences of female infanticide and female foeticide have been noted. As late as 1984, the investigations of the Women's Federation revealed an alarming disparity between the number of male and female infants, the main cause being 'female infanticide, under the influence of male chauvinism, which was a vestige of feudal ideology'. The report also added that in one of the counties in China more than forty female infants had been drowned in 1980–81 (Ramanathan, 1997).

Violation of rights of women to mobility and to define their identify

The extent to which women can themselves define their identity, mobility, style of dressing, post-marital residence and sexual preference, varies across regions, countries and districts/councils within countries. Kinship and marriage patterns, norms governed by religion, ethnicity, caste, class and marital status all have a bearing on the extent to which women enjoy the ability to practise this right. However, with the rise in fundamentalism, even fundamentalists groups are having a say on these aspects. In Afghanistan, the Taliban (when in power) issued an order against free movement of women, women dressing without covering their heads, driving cars, girl children going to schools, and so on (Afghan Mission, 1998). In New Delhi, the Bharatiya Janata Party mooted the idea of evolving a policy directive against girls wearing skirts to school, as they believed that it went against 'Indian' traditions. Fortunately, it was vetoed at the last minute. With the rise in Hindu fundamentalism in India, Indian women are being increasingly pushed back into traditional patriarchal norms. In some of the Moslem-dominated CIS countries, with the re-emergence of patriarchal norms which were kept suppressed throughout the socialist era, a similar pattern has been observed. If passed by the Senate, the recent Bill passed by the lower house on Islamisation of the legal system in Pakistan may portend negative consequences for women.

A cause of concern for those involved in poverty alleviation is the evidence that with increase in income of the upper caste Hindu and Muslim men in parts of South Asia, women are pulled out of the labour force and restrictions are placed on their mobility and autonomy (Kabeer, 1997). Thus if gender concerns are not addressed in poverty reduction strategies, women may lose on their rights or status in society as individuals.

Domestic violence against women

Domestic violence against women has existed from time immemorial. But it is only as recent as the 1993 World Human Rights Conference that violence against women in the family was recognised as a violation of women's human rights. Violence against women takes different forms. Throughout Asia and the CIS, cases of wife beating, girl child abuse, and marital rape have been reported. Domestic violence is not restricted to lower income households, but exists also in middle and upper income households.

In South Asia violence against women begins even before their birth. Child marriage is popular in most of South Asia, especially in the rural areas. The practice of dowry is widely prevalent, and is spreading even to matrilineal communities. Even in Kerala (South India) where a significant level of human development among women exists, instances of dowry deaths and suicide of women are on the rise. Killing of brides for not bringing adequate dowry is also prevalent in certain parts of India, Pakistan, Bangladesh and Nepal (Jahan, 1998, Rosa, 1995, UNICEF, 1996). Dowry deaths are noted to be on the rise in some pockets of South Asia, like the Terai belt in Nepal. The ancient practice of *Sati* is still to disappear in Rajasthan. Wife beating is not only common, but studies have revealed that the average South Asian man thinks it is his right to beat his wife, and many women accept this (ICRW, 1998).

In South-East Asia, domestic violence is very much common, and noted to have increased in some countries. Even the 'high human development' (HD) countries like Singapore and Malaysia record cases of marital rape and wife battering (Darium, 1993). In Cambodia (low in HD), though spousal abuse existed in the pre-war period, today it is estimated to be much higher than earlier (ADB, 1996). Though studies have attributed this post-war increase in domestic violence to the participation of Cambodian men in war,[11] such psycho-social arguments ignore the inherent power relations between men and women in society. In Mongolia domestic violence against women has been noted to have increased.

Other forms of domestic violence have also been noted in the region. In Cambodia, Vietnam and Thailand, poor families at times force young girls to engage in prostitution, to economically help their families. In China (East Asia) cases of female infanticide and foeticide have been observed, and have perhaps increased with the one-child per family norm. In Indonesia and Malaysia, cases of female genital mutilation continue to be recorded, causing injury to women, as well as repressing their sexual desires.

In the CIS countries domestic violence against women has increased with the rise in unemployment and economic insecurity among both males and females. In Ukraine and Russia alcoholism and wife beating are on the rise. Mental harassment of women has also increased. A popular belief in Ukraine goes that men hit their wives because they 'love' them (Teslenko, 1995). Rates of divorce and suicides have increased due to the economic and social crisis, with suicide rates being higher among men. This phenomenon has been less prevalent among Moslem communities in Central Asia because of the strong community norms binding the family and kinship together (Carlson, 1994).

Part of the problem is the existence of legal barriers with regard to domestic violence. In Russia marital rape is not considered a criminal offence unless the wife is judicially separated from the husband at the time of rape. In other instances, the law may be supportive, but the judges who interpret the law may be biased. There are cases where the legislation may be in place, but its interpretation could be flawed. For instance, in Bangladesh, dowry is legally banned and dowry deaths have heavy penalty. But quite often men get away with the crime because of the attitude of the judiciary. There are also cases where the community intervenes to prevent justice from being meted out, as in the case of the rape of a woman activist (employee in the government of India) who prevented a child marriage from taking place. As observed by Dr Radhika Coomaraswamy, the attitude that 'what happens in the home is a private affair and the law should intervene only if it becomes a public affair' pervades the judiciary, police, community and family at all levels (Arunatilaka, 1997).

Violations of rights of women during conflicts and war.

During war, women are often left to fend for themselves and their children, while their husbands are conscripted. Violence against women by the opposition groups has been observed in many cases. Women's bodies become sites on which groups in opposition choose to demonstrate their powers. For example, during the Soviet actions in Afghanistan between 1979 and 1988, women Afghan rebels were imprisoned in a jail in Kabul, tortured, raped and even impregnated in some cases (cited in Wali, 1998). When women take refuge or leave the place, their problems do not end. Not only are they subject to economic discrimination, but also subject to other forms of human rights violations. They become the target of large-scale terror campaigns, mass/multiple rapes, abduction, torture, forced impregnation, and trafficking in women. At times they are forced to extend sexual favours in order to access food and basic services for themselves and their children. Men in refugee camps tend to be much less occupied than women who have to look after children and attend to other routine chores. Increase in arguments and violence against women, when compared to their pre-refugee situation, have been noted. Relief agencies are often not gender sensitive; and do not respond to these strategic gender concerns.

Custodial violence against women

On the issue of custodial violence against women, very little empirical data could be gathered other than from Pakistan and India. In Pakistan the number of women in custody has increased. Women are incarcerated for many reasons, some of which violate international human rights law. For example, penal laws that criminalise sexual intercourse outside marriage are routinely applied to imprison women who have committed adultery, as well as women who are victims of rape. According to human rights lawyers, more than 70 per cent of women in police custody experience not only physical abuse but are also sexually abused by their jailers (Human

Rights Watch, 1998). In India too, incidences of custodial violence have been noted both on women who have been imprisoned, as well as female relatives of male prisoners. The rape of Mathura by the police in Maharashtra in the 1980s received a lot of attention from women's groups, leading to changes in legislation on custodial violence (Gandhi and Shah, 1991, Gangoli, 1996).

Violence against women in market and public places

With the trend towards privatisation, there has been a marked increase in violation of women's rights within market-related organisations: EPZs, private hospitals, private education institutions and so on. Instances of economic exploitation at the work place have already been highlighted in the previous section. But different forms of social exploitation are also becoming apparent. In EPZs, for example, women employees are at times expected to extend sexual favours to renew contracts, or to be granted promotion. Overt sexual harassment is also not uncommon. A 'pseudo culture' of applying makeup, beauty competitions, and Christmas parties is often introduced in EPZs to distract workers from these conditions.

Women fishworkers constitute another group whose rights are often violated, not just economically but also socially. Their active role in vending fish, often takes them outside the home. While this has enhanced their mobility and access to income (though not control), women fishworkers are more vulnerable to violence at the work place than women in most other rural occupations. Instances of harassment within buses and rape and sexual harassment at fish markets are often reported in parts of India. In spite of the fact that women fishworkers spend a substantial time away from home, the responsibility of domestic work, child care and care of the elderly invariably falls on them. Thus their working hours are also long.

In China, sexual harassment during medical examinations has been noted, both in private and government hospitals. This may well be common in other countries as well. With the spread of higher education, sexual harassment of girl students has come to light. In Chennai (India) for example, a few cases of sexual harassment of MPhil and PhD girl students by their guides came to light a few years back. Some of them were forced to leave the programme in between, while others decided to comply. Eve teasing in college campuses is well known in India. It is not just the work place, schools and hospitals which are sites of violence, but also public spaces like streets, cinema halls and entertainment zones. Rape in public places has been on the rise, but this could also be due to the increase in rates of reporting.

(Apart from these 9 violations there are in addition, two more which have already been examined in detail in the preceding chapter. They are: *Violation of women's rights to decision-making;* and *Violation of women's rights to land, assets and other resources.*)

Conclusion

This overview of the situation of human rights reveals that in spite of ratifying CEDAW and guaranteeing equality on the basis of gender, the governments of the Asian and CIS countries have not only been unable to safeguard women's rights within the household, community and markets, but in some instances they have themselves violated women's human rights. Women's human rights are thus ignored in all institutional sites. The overview also reveals the presence of a few legal loopholes, especially with regard to domestic violence, which need to be addressed. A more thorough analysis is definitely required. In some cases, the legislation may be pro-women, but its interpretation may vary depending on the gender sensitivity of the person. In few cases, community and family norms may come in the way of the effective use of legislation. Thus protecting and promoting women's human rights require changes in their rules, norms, people and distribution of power in all institutions of society. In spite of the undemocratic nature of many of the former socialist regimes, they were, on the whole, better than the liberal democratic ones at protecting and promoting women's economic rights and rights to decision-making.

The observations are also that human rights violations against women take certain gender-specific forms, such as forced pregnancy, forced virginity exams, or they primarily target girls/women with female infanticide, female foeticide, wife beating, rape, forced sterilisation and forced trafficking of women for purposes of sexual servitude (Human Rights Watch, 1998). However, at the same time one cannot categorise all women into one category. Dalit women in India face certain gender- and caste-specific discrimination, like forced religious prostitution and lack of rights to public decision-making. Women belonging to ethnic/racial minorities are oppressed by gender as well as their ethnic/racial identity. There is hence a need to focus not just on equality between men and women of a particular group, but equality between those of different groups as well. Women's human rights cannot be promoted and protected unless all forms of inequalities and human rights violations are addressed (Kapur, R, 1997).

The overview also offers insights on the recent debates about 'individual' rights vs 'collective rights' of people. The proponents of the 'collective rights' of people have argued that the concept of rights of 'individuals' which is popular in the West, fosters individualism and ignores the collective rights of people, like rights to Common Property Resources (CPRs), rights to preserve culture and so on. In Asia, some of the politicians who wish to keep out the influence and power of the West from their countries, have used the concept of 'collective-rights' to argue the case for preserving Asian values.

But the preceding evidence shows that there is no one unified set of 'Asian values', and these values (like western values) are not necessarily progressive towards women. The recent discourse on Asian values and how it needs to be protected may remain a powerful challenge to anything that is remotely subversive of existing power relations. One therefore needs to ensure that any effort to talk of collective rights is not hijacked by the dominant forces (ibid, 1997). Promoting individual rights of women and collective rights which do not erode the individual rights is therefore important.

End Notes

1. Rampant abuses against women have traditionally been excused or ignored. Rape in situations of conflict by combatants is prohibited under international humanitarian law but until recently was dismissed as part of the inevitable 'spoils of war'. Domestic violence was regarded as a 'private' matter only, and not as a crime that the state must prosecute and punish.

2. Korean women aged between 12 and 20 were forced, kidnapped, lured or deceived, to service the sexual needs of the Japanese military in their occupied regions and fields of war before and during World War II. The total number of victims is estimated to be between 70,000 and 2,00,000, of whom 80 to 90% were women taken from Korea. In 1994 the Japanese government mooted a proposal to raise non-governmental funds through private donations for the Comfort Women by which compensation would be provided for the victims. In February 1996, Radhika Coomaraswamy, special rapporteur to the UN Commission on Human Rights, made a strong recommendation to the Commission that the Japanese government should be held legally responsible for compensation to be made to victims of the sexual slavery system.

3. According to one estimate, between 1,00,000 and 2,00,000 Nepali girls have been trafficked. Most of them go to India (Fernando, 1998).

4. A study on domestic violence conducted in Cambodia observed that one of the problems in countries which are emerging from long periods of civil war was that men who have been in military duty knew nothing but violence throughout their lives, and tended to repeat the same pattern within the family.

Chapter Five

Emerging Vulnerable Groups and Issues: Gender, Poverty, Human Rights

Vulnerable Groups and their Location

It is possible to identify 20 groups of women who may need to be focussed upon. A mapping of these groups and their possible spatial location is presented in Table 5.1. Cutting across regions, a few groups of women in poverty/women subject to human rights violations can be identified. These include women in marginal and small farming households, women in environmentally fragile areas, women artisanal fishworkers (coastal belts), women from ethnic minorities, disabled women, women in the urban informal sector, girl children, women refugees, sex workers, women affected by AIDS and women subject to domestic violence.

Table 5.1: Vulnerable Groups and their Location

Group	Sub-region/country
Particular sections of Women Headed Households	<ul><li>All over the region, but not all WHH</li><li>Widows in north-western and north-central India and Nepal from low income groups, as well as abandoned widows from any income group</li><li>War widows in Vietnam, Cambodia and PDR of Laos</li></ul>

	• Single women/unwed mothers in the CIS countries
Women landless labourers	South Asia, Indonesia and Thailand
Women bonded labourers	South Asia
Women in marginal and small farming households	South Asia, China, Vietnam, Cambodia, PDR of Laos, Myanmar, Indonesia, Philippines and Thailand
Small herders involved in livestock rearing	Mongolia
Women dispossessed of land	Vietnam, Cambodia, China, and possibly Kyrgyzstan and Tajikistan
Women bonded labourers	South Asia in particular
Women artisanal fishworkers	• Coastal areas of India, Bangladesh, Sri Lanka and Maldives • Coastal areas of the Philippines, Indonesia, Thailand and Vietnam in South-East Asia • Coastal areas of China
Women from ethnic minorities/ Scheduled Castes	• Gurun, Magar, Tamang, Limbu and Rai in Nepal, aborigines of the Terai • Dalits in India and Nepal • Tamil women and men in northern and eastern Sri Lanka • All ethnic minorities in PDR of Laos and Vietnam • Muslim women in the Philippines • Ethnic minorities in China found in border and backward areas (ethnic minorities from China in other South-East Asia countries are often not poor, but are discriminated against)
Women in human poverty from non-poor households	• North-western and north-central India (in particular UP, Punjab and Haryana) • Baluchistan, north-western frontier and Sind of Pakistan • Far western hills and mountains, and central hills

Women in backward and environmentally fragile areas	• Interior provinces of the western region in China • Gobi desert in Mongolia • BIMARU belt in India • North-eastern and southern Bangladesh • North and eastern part of Sri Lanka • Rural South Punjab and Baluchistan in Pakistan • Central Terai, Central Mountains and far western hills in Nepal • North and north-eastern in Thailand • Upland areas and Luzon in the Philippines • Northern highlands, north-central coastal strip and central highlands in Vietnam • Central region in PDR of Laos and Rural Cambodia • Rural Java and outer islands in Indonesia • Parts of Myanmar • South of the region, rural cities of Osh, Naryn, D Jalalabad and Talas in Kyrgyzstan • Kurgenteppe in southern part and Garm and Kuluab region in central part of Tajikistan • Earthquake zones and border areas in Armenia • Nakhichevan in Azerbaijan
Urban women in the informal sector	• Indonesia, Philippines, Thailand • India, Bangladesh, Sri Lanka, Nepal • China
Women in EPZs*	• South-East Asia: the Philippines, Indonesia, Thailand, Malaysia, • East Asia: Korea, China • South Asia: Sri Lanka, Bangladesh, India
Women sex workers*	• South-East Asia: Thailand, Vietnam, Cambodia, Myanmar and PDR of Laos • South Asia: Nepal, Bangladesh, Pakistan and India

Migrant domestic workers*	• The Philippines, Thailand, Indonesia • Sri Lanka
Retrenched/displaced women workers in the formal sector*	• South-East Asia: Thailand, Indonesia, Malasyia, Vietnam, the Philippines • East Asia: Republic of Korea • CIS: All countries
Women refugees and internally displaced persons	• Tamils in Sri Lanka • Myanmar refugees in Bangladesh • Tibetan/Bhutani refugees in Nepal • Refugees from all over South Asia in India and also Tibetan refugees • Myanmar refugees in Thailand and Vietnam • Afghans in Central Asia • Displaced groups in Armenia, Azerbaijan, Georgia
Disabled women/girls and orphans from income poor families	• All countries • Especially Vietnam, Cambodia, and PDR of Laos • Sri Lanka
Elderly women	• All countries, less in South Asia (abandoned and elderly women from low income groups) • In Central Asia and other CIS countries (also single elderly women)
Women in large and young families	• Central Asia and other CIS countries
Girl Children	• CIS countries • South Asia • Street children from slums/trafficked children in Bangkok, Manila, Jakarta, Bombay, Calcutta, Kathmandu, Dhaka, Karachi
Female infants and foetus*	• Vietnam and China with respect to education • India and Nepal • China
Women affected by HIV/AIDS[1]*	• South-East Asia: Thailand, Vietnam, Cambodia, Myanmar • South Asia: India and Nepal

* *Implies that all members of this group may not be poor, but violations of socio-cultural-political rights may be high.*

There are also sub-regional and country specific groups

In South Asia where there is a high degree of landlessness and bonded labour, women in landless households and women in bondage constitute a particularly vulnerable group. Specific to South Asia, another group in poverty are the scheduled castes. Women in non-poor households who are subject to extreme forms of gender discrimination, may constitute a key group, subject to different forms of human rights violations. Some of them, particularly widows, may also be in poverty. Girl children in South Asia require added attention in all spheres compared to other regions. Women sex workers in India and Nepal who cater to clients from low income groups constitute a key group in poverty. Though migrant domestic workers from Sri Lanka and women in EPZs in Sri Lanka, India and Bangladesh are not necessarily poor, they are subject to different forms of human rights violations.

In South-East Asian countries under transition, women war widows dispossessed of land as a result of the reform may constitute a key group in poverty. Women workers displaced through reform, as well as through loss of access to markets of the former USSR are another group in poverty. While disability is a global phenomenon, the prolonged war has lead to a higher rate of disability among women compared to the other sub-regions, and they require specific attention. Girl children require specific attention with regard to education. Sex workers from this sub-region, who often operate across the border (with neighbouring South-East Asian countries), tend to be poorer than their counterparts in capitalist South-East Asia and need to be addressed.

In capitalist South-East Asia, specially in those countries classified as Priority 2, elderly women, middle-aged sex workers, women retrenched as a result of the economic crisis, illegal migrant domestic workers, women in the informal sector and girl children on the streets constitute key groups in poverty. Though all sex workers in this sub-region are not poor, they are subject to different forms of human rights violations. This also applies to women working in EPZs. These two groups need specific attention in this sub-region.

In China in East Asia, women dispossessed of land, women landless labourers, women in the urban informal sector (including migrant women), unskilled women workers in SEEZs and elderly women constitute key groups in poverty. Girl children are subject to different forms of human rights violation with respect to education and health, and female infants/foetuses in certain pockets are not allowed to survive. These groups may require specific attention. **In Mongolia,** small herders and the urban informal sector workers who may be poorer than their rural counterparts, constitute a group in poverty. In the high human development East Asian countries like **the Republic of Korea,** human rights violations against women workers are a concern, though they may not constitute a group in poverty.

In some of the CIS countries, unlike Asia, urban poverty may be as high as rural poverty. Women at the lower rungs who have been retrenched, single young women with children, women with large families, elderly women living on their own, rural women dispossesed of land with de-collectivisation and women in the informal industrial and service sectors constitute key groups in poverty. While the income status of sex workers is little known, they do constitute a group subject to different forms of human rights abuse.

Emerging Issues and Possible Strategies

Emerging out of the analysis on gender-specific causes of poverty and human rights violations against women, almost all the issues that follow are relevant across the different regions/sub-regions. However, specific issues/aspects of each issue may require more attention in a particular region or sub-region. Though many of these issues/sub-issues are interlinked and hence difficult to separate, some of them may be more important than the others in terms of their impact on poverty and women's human rights. The importance of different issues is explored here at greater length, both in terms of centrality to addressing poverty and human rights concerns of women and in terms of regions in which they may be important.

Women's independent rights to productive resources and capital

Productive resources include land, livestock and credit (depending on how it is used). Among these resources, perhaps women's rights to land is particularly important as it also has a bearing on the ability to rear livestock, and the quantum of credit which can be absorbed. Studies have shown that those without land are able to absorb less quantum of credit and rear less number of livestock than those with land (Murthy and Rao, 1997).

Focusing on the issue of women's rights to land is particularly important in those sub-regions/countries governed by a patrilineal system of inheritance like in South Asia (except communities indicated), China, Vietnam and Cambodia after de-collectivisation, and perhaps some of the CIS countries. Even in some of the so-called matrilineal communities of South Asia, ownership of land does not mean control. In such cases as well there is a need to promote women's rights to land. The issues of rights to credit and extension services are cross-cutting issues, and need to be addressed in all the regions/sub-regions. Though not as central as the issue of land rights, it is perhaps easier to operationalise.

Some of the key strategies which could be adopted to expand women's rights to land include:
- Promoting legal reform, pertaining to women's independent or joint rights to land for women.
- Promoting legal measures to protect women's rights to land during de-collectivisation.
- Documenting examples of successful cases where women have claimed their existing rights to land collectively and individually.

- Monitoring implementation and impact of policies to accord women rights to land as part of government schemes, as well as impacting of macro-economic policies and infrastructural projects on women's existing rights to land.
- Expanding women's participation in decision-making in traditional community structures, local self-governance institutions and all input and marketing cooperatives, and enhancing resources at the disposal of the last two institutions.
- Promoting joint ownership of land or women's independent ownership of land as part of agricultural programmes of all field projects of NGOs.
- Strengthening non-governmental channels of credit for women.

Women's rights to education, health care and child care

Ensuring women's rights to education, health care and child care is of course important in all the countries listed as Priorities 1 and 2.

Among these, women's rights to education is particularly important, as it is highly instrumental for accruing gains in other spheres. The regional analysis of access to education suggests that promoting women and girl children's right to education is a critical issue in South Asia, where literacy levels are low, and marked intra-household inequalities persist where access to education is concerned. Another set of countries where attention may be needed on female education is South-East Asia/East Asia countries under transition like Vietnam, Cambodia, the PDR of Laos and China where cuts and privatisation have led to the resurfacing of gender bias in education. South-East Asian countries affected by economic crisis is another sub-region where rights of girls to education may need to be protected; in particular Indonesia, where poverty levels were expected to double by the end of the last century. While exact implications of the transition in the CIS countries on women's access to education is not clear, particular attention may need to be placed on Tajikistan, Kyrgyzstan, Uzbekistan and Azerbaijan; where Islamic fundamentalism is noted to be on the rise.

A similar regional prioritisation may be required in the sphere of women's rights to health care. However, women's rights to health is a key issue in almost all the CIS countries falling under Priorities 1 and 2, as along with transition, the government's health care system has taken a back seat, and there is a steep rise in MMRs. Though child care is important across the different regions and sub-regions, it is particularly important to address this issue in the former CIS countries where state provision of child care has collapsed. In contrast to the analysis on education, child care may be particularly required by women in Christian-dominated CIS countries (Armenia, Georgia and Moldova), falling under Priority 1 where the nuclear family is the common norm.

To promote women's rights to education, health and child care (especially in South Asia, South-East Asia under transition and under economic crisis and the CIS), the following strategies could be considered:

- Strengthening networks of NGOs at the national and sub-regional level which monitor and analyse the budgets of governments and allocation of aid by international agencies with the viewpoint of promoting greater and appropriate resource allocation to education, health and child care.
- Advocating increase in proportion of government/aid budget allocated for health, education, child care and basic services to reach the UN target of 20 per cent.
- Advocating appropriate intra-sectoral and intra-spatial/regional allocation of resources within the health and education budget.
- Advocating/enhancing proportion of women staff in government at all levels.
- Advocating gender sensitivity of health, education and child care personnel and services.
- Strengthening non-governmental/community managed provision of appropriate health, education and child care services in Priority 1 countries.

- Strengthening non-governmental/community managed programmes for the disabled in countries wherein they form a significant proportion of the population, and mainstream concerns of the disabled.

Women's rights to social/gender-just trading practices, capital flows and technology

Globalisation is a reality, and over the coming years the move towards globalisation is more likely to accelerate than decelerate. Though the process may open up few opportunities for women, on the whole it is likely to have an adverse impact on the lives of poor women. In this context, it is important for poor women to be able to make use of the opportunities coming up, and protect themselves against negative consequences like, loss of access to productive land-based resources, marine resources, jobs, employment and income, increasing food insecurity, reduced access to medicines and appropriation of indigenous knowledge. This can be done by expanding women's rights to productive assets and capital and investment in basic education and child care and at the same time, promoting strategies to protect poor women against negative consequences. The problem may need to be addressed at two levels: at the level of symptoms, and also at the level of trade structures and rules which are anti-poor and anti-women. Intervening at these two levels is particularly urgent in the context of countries whose GDP is significantly dependent on trade and capital flows (capitalist South-East Asia, Sri Lanka, Moldova,[2]), and which are considerably dependent on import of grains for meeting minimum calorific requirements (Sri Lanka, Indonesia, China, Bangladesh, the Philippines, Malaysia, Pakistan, the PDR of Laos, Afghanistan[3]).

The key strategies which may be required include:
- Advocating a separate Committee on Trade and Gender within WTO, ASEAN, APEC and SAARC and promote human rights and gender equitable standards in international trade,[4] while

at the same time ensuring that the clause is not used against the interest of developing countries.
- Strengthening formation/strengthening of regional networks of NGOs and trade unions on the issue of gender and trade, and their advocacy strategies at ministerial conferences held at sub-regional/regional/international levels.
- Strengthening alternative fair trading networks in the sub-regions/region.
- Strengthening support services for those displaced by trade so that they can find alternative avenues for employment.
- Advocating adoption of ILO standards to unskilled international migrant workers, EPZ workers and home-based/contract workers, and strengthening the monitoring of adherence to these standards.
- Strengthening/promoting bi-lateral agreements between countries which send/receive migrant women in large numbers to protect the rights and security of migrants.
- Raising awareness among consumers on gender-just trade, and promote their linkages with trade unions and third world networks.
- Registering indigenous practices under TRIPs, and report appropriation of indigenous knowledge of women under TRIPs.
- Advocating adoption of Tobin Tax on trade and its utilisation for development of women.
- Strengthening the access of women entrepreneurs/workers in the informal sectors to technology and support services so that they can re-orient their output to export opportunities.
- Strengthening efforts to improve regulation of international financial markets to stem panics like the one in South-East Asia.

Women's rights to food security

The analysis of the impact of trade and environmental degradation points to the urgent need for prioritising the issue of food security. This has a direct bearing on women's ability to ensure their survival and that of their families. In fact, food insecurity is going to become more acute in the coming years due to a combination of several factors linked with the impact of these two trends: *saturation of possibility of expanding land under cultivation* (in some places), *decrease in cultivable land due to diversion for non-farm use, decrease in farm land under food grains, lowering of productivity due to soil erosion, declining of water tables and saturation of gains from fertiliser use, increase in amount diverted for animal feed, decrease in catch of fish due to depletion of marine resources, increase in food prices due to food scarcity, as well as removal of subsidies to farmers* and consumers, and *a higher rate of population growth than agricultural production*. As discussed earlier, decline in food security is bound to have a greater impact on poor women rather than poor men, on landless labourers and marginal farmers rather than the big farmers, and on urban poor rather than the rural poor.

Though across Asia and the CIS, promoting women's rights to food security is a major issue, it is particularly important to strengthen food security in those countries which fall or are likely to fall below the food import dependency threshold like in Sri Lanka, Bangladesh, Pakistan and Afghanistan in South Asia, China (also Republic of Korea and Korea DPR) in East Asia, Indonesia and the Philippines and the PDR of Laos in South-East Asia. Though data on the CIS countries which fall below the import threshold were not available, food production is likely to fall drastically in Kazakhstan (now a net importer of wheat) due to soil erosion and sudden loss of the former USSR market (Brown, 1997).

In this context, some of the key strategies which could be adopted to strengthen women's rights to food security in the region include (also see IFAD, 1995):
- Advocacy to promote trade policies which strengthen food security, including dismantling of subsidies and trade barriers

among developed countries, regulating supply of food grains for animal feed, and maintaining a reserve global stock to meet emergencies.

- Advocacy to prevent agricultural land for other purposes especially in food importing countries.
- Strengthening efforts to conserve water, soil and marine resources, to identify indigenous methods of controlling pest attacks, and to evolve low cost grain storage structures.
- Strengthening women's land rights and participation in decision-making with regard to agriculture and fisheries resources.
- Strengthening incentive systems for farmers so that they place priority on food security.
- Strengthening strategies to prevent distress sales, hoarding of food grains, and corruption in public distribution systems.
- Strengthening early warning systems which could be used by women with regard to drought and famine.
- Strengthening protection of indigenous knowledge of women and men pertaining to seeds, organic manure, pest control, etc., under the TRIPS.
- Disseminating information kits providing practical information and resource materials on how NGOs could strengthen food security with the active leadership of women.

Women's rights to work at just wages and terms and women's right to rest

The analysis of gender-specific causes of poverty revealed that a very important variable which determines women's status within their families and their ability to access household resources like food, health care and training is their contribution to family income in cash. Increasing this contribution is important in all the countries within both the regions, but is particularly important in Pakistan, Bangladesh and India in South Asia where women's contribution is less than 25 per cent. Though not a country of priority as far as poverty goes, women's contribution also needs to be enhanced in the Republic of Korea and Hong Kong under Chinese control. Given that across regions and countries women are responsible for domestic work and child care, promoting an equitable gender division of domestic labour needs to be addressed in all of Asia and the CIS.

To enhance women's rights to work with just and equal wages, and to rest (adapting from Braun, J V, 1995), the following strategies could be considered:

- Promote ratification of all ILO Conventions related to Labour (in particular Convention No. 100 pertaining to equal remuneration) by those countries which are yet to do so.
- Country level legal reform towards employment guarantee for women and men, equal wages for work of equal value,[5] and just terms and conditions including child care provision.
- Strengthen efforts to monitor implementation of legislation/ promotion of networks.
- Strengthen gender sensitivity of trade unions and exclusive trade unions for women workers.
- Advocate gender-specific social clause in global and/or regional trade pertaining to employment and wages. Advocate adequate compensation in the case of retrenchment of women (MNCs and local industries).
- Promote alternative sources of employment which guarantee just wages.
- Strengthen efforts to increase productivity and labour absorption capacity of agriculture, and non-farm employment opportunities for women.
- Strengthen efforts for development of technologies to reduce women's work burden, as well as increase male sharing of domestic work and child care.

Women's rights to CPRs and participation in Natural Resource Management

Women's rights to common property resources like forests, wasteland, tank, marine resources, and their participation in conservation and replenishment of these resources is another issue that needs to be focused upon. Considering the depletion of common property resources and dilution of women's access to these due to privatisation and commercialisation, these issues need to be tackled urgently in all the countries of the region.

Promoting women's rights to forests and participation in afforestation programmes may be particularly important in the Philippines, Indonesia, Malaysia and Thailand in South-East Asia, Mongolia in East Asia, Pakistan and Bangladesh in South Asia which have experienced above two per cent per annum rates of deforestation. Soil erosion may need to be addressed in the CIS countries where soil erosion is high, while conservation of groundwater resources is urgent in Punjab and Rajasthan (India) and the northern parts of China. Efforts to promote class and gender equity in access to ground water is another issue which will need to be addressed. River bank erosion and siltation may, in particular, need to be addressed along the Mekong River in South-East Asia. Conservation of marine resources is important in the coastal belts of South-East Asia and China.

The following strategies may be required to protect CPRs and promote women's rights:
- Monitor implementation of Agenda 21 agreed upon in the UN Conference on Environment and Development in 1992, with particular reference to clauses pertaining to women and indigenous communities.
- Strengthen monitoring of environmental violations by multinationals and local industries in Priorities 1 and 2 countries,

and bring it to the notice of the Trade and Environment Committee of the WTO.
- Advocate policies to ensure equal rights of women to CPRs (forests, wasteland, water) and their benefits.
- Study the relationship between gender and environment in the context of each of its field operations in priority countries, and evolve plans on the basis of that.
- Advocate/promote sustainable development practices in the priority countries.
- Enhance participation of women in committees to manage CPRs, and ownership of community assets created through these initiatives.
- Disseminate information kits providing practical information and resource materials on how NGOs can address gender issues in NRM in different priority countries.

Women's rights to political participation and gender-just governance

Promoting women's rights to political participation and their ability to use the expanded space to further the (gender, race, class, ethnic and caste) interests of women are particularly important. Increasing representation of women in Parliament is a value by itself, and also leads to instrumental gains for women wherever they have crossed a threshold level. The presence of over 33 per cent women in Sweden and Norway contributed to the passing of several gender-sensitive policies and legislation. However, the link need not be automatic wherever women have internalised many patriarchal values in society, and where women's caste, class, ethnic and religious interests supersede gender interests as in the case of South Asia. Thus bottom up efforts towards empowerment of women from the marginalised group, and sensitisation of women and men representatives to gender and social concerns are as important as arguing the case for women's representation.

The representation of women in Parliament needs to be improved particularly in South Asia where they hold only 6.9 per cent of the seats. Though women's representation is slightly higher amongst the South-East Asian countries (averaging 11.1 per cent) and China (21 per cent), it is still below the minimum threshold of 33 per cent recommended by researchers in order to have an impact on the legislative outcome (see UNDP, 1997, Table 3). Though data on the CIS countries could not be accessed, women's representation is noted to have declined in the process of transition.

Some of the strategies which could be adopted towards this end include:
- Legal reform towards 33 per cent reservation for women in all kinds of public decision-making fora.
- Protect women's rights to political participation in the countries of the CIS.
- Strengthen provision of credit for poor women to contest elections.
- Strengthen legal space for women to organise and protest, especially in authoritarian regimes.
- Strengthen gender sensitisation efforts directed at male and female elected members at different levels.
- Strengthen accountability of politicians and the bureaucracy to poor women and their concerns.
- Strengthen regional and sub-regional level networking on political participation: formal and informal processes, in particular which try to influence manifestos from a gender perspective.
- Document successful strategies adopted in the region.

Women's reproductive rights

Expanding women's rights to determine whether to have children, the number of children to have, when to conceive, and also whether to have children within or outside the institution of marriage are other issues which need attention. At the same time, it is necessary to ensure that women make informed choices, which are not against the interests of female foetuses and female infants. Expanding women's rights to decide on contraception and access to safe contraception are also important. Enhancing their ability to negotiate with male partners to use condoms and contraception is another issue.

Expanding women's reproductive rights is especially important in South Asia. Here family and kinship structures pull women in one direction, inflicting compulsory motherhood, and continued reproduction till the wish for sons is fulfilled, while state policies pull them in another (one child per family). This is also essential in countries like China and Singapore where the government regulates women's reproductive behaviour in a top–down manner through either restricting or increasing women's reproductive activities.

Some of the strategies which need to be adopted to further women's reproductive rights include:

- Legal reform to recognise violations of reproductive rights such as virginity tests, forced abortion, forced sterilisation, forced pregnancy and female genital mutilation as a crime.
- Strengthening efforts to highlight and prevent violation of women's reproductive rights by the state, religious institutions, family members and others.
- Strengthening efforts of networks to highlight and curb harmful reproductive technologies targeted at women, and promote use of safe contraceptives/indigenous methods amongst men and women.
- Strengthening integration of basic reproductive health care [including services for sexually transmitted diseases (STDs)] in existing health services, and expand proportion of women staff in reproductive health care.
- Strengthening provision of reproductive health care to sex workers.

Women's rights to freedom from violence

Women's lack of rights to land in some countries, lack of rights to just wages, lack of reproductive rights and lack of rights to political participation are the more invisible forms of violence against women. In addition, it is necessary to work towards elimination of the more visible forms of violence against women and girl children in the family, work place and the broader public space, such as wife beating, sexual abuse, girl child abuse, female foeticide and infanticide, dowry harassment and so on. While violence against women is all pervasive, and requires attention across the different regions and sub-regions, some forms of violence may be specific to particular sub-regions/countries. For example, specific strategies to address the issue of dowry-related violence, the devadasi system, and witch hunting are required in South Asia. Female infanticide and feoticide need to be eliminated in South Asia, China and the Republic of Korea. The practice of female genital mutilation needs to end in some of the Muslim-dominated countries of Asia and the CIS.

Transforming ideologies which surround these practices, as well as uplifting the low economic position of women are essential. Some of the other strategies which may be essential to create spaces free from violence against women include:

- Strengthening the monitoring of the articles in CEDAW pertaining to domestic violence.
- Strengthening efforts to sensitise judges, prosecutors, police officers, jail and prison personnel on gender and violence.
- Strengthening international law on asylum for women victims of violence due to gender-specific socio-cultural norms.
- Legal reforms a) recognising domestic violence against women as a crime, b) recognising violence against women during wars as a war crime, c) criminalising violence during custody by prison or jail officials, d) putting the onus of proof of innocence on the perpetrator in violence against women.

- Providing support for temporary shelter homes and livelihood activities for victims of domestic violence who wish to explore alternative living arrangements.

Promoting and Protecting the Rights of Sex-workers[6]

In the context of increase in trafficking of women for sexual purposes in the 1990s, it is necessary to evolve strategies to provide people in poverty-stricken areas and community (especially with a history of sending girls into prostitution) with other economic options, so that women are not forced into this profession. At the same time, strategies to promote and protect the rights of those who are already in the profession are necessary.

Like domestic violence, the problem of trafficking of women seems to be all pervasive, and needs to be addressed everywhere. However, specific pockets seem more vulnerable to prostitution and may need more attention. Thailand, Vietnam, Cambodia, and the PDR of Laos in South-East Asia and Nepal and India in South Asia are examples.

The strategies which may be required to prevent sex work and promote and protect the rights of sex workers include:

- Strengthening poverty alleviation efforts in the belts where trafficking is concentrated, and among communities forced into this profession in South Asia.
- Strengthening dissemination of information on practices related to trafficking to warn local communities in vulnerable areas.
- Strengthening presence of international security forces in vulnerable border areas.
- Legal reform to prevent victimisation of sex workers (women and girl children) and to promote penalisation of perpetrators.
- Strengthening training of women sex workers on their rights, and sensitivity and skills of border forces, police, judges and other relevant officials.
- Strengthening efforts to provide services to improve living conditions of sex workers (in particular health care).

- Strengthening efforts of organisations to rehabilitate sex workers who want to leave the trade, and equip these women with skills in alternative IGPs.
- Strengthening co-ordination/ongoing efforts of networks working on this area, and extend their outreach to the countries of the CIS.

Women's rights to peace and harmony

Apart from freedom from violence, like men, women too, require an environment of peace and harmony. In times of unrest (communal or otherwise) women are affected in gender-specific ways. Strategies are therefore required to promote peace and prevent conflicts, as well as address gender-specific implications of conflicts.

There are pockets in almost every country in Asia and the CIS which are in some form of strife. Incidence of conflicts are particularly high in Afghanistan, and parts of Sri Lanka, India, Pakistan and Bhutan in South Asia, Myanmar and parts of Indonesia in South-East Asia, and Armenia, Azerbaijan and Georgia in the CIS. In China and the Republic of Korea, lack of space to organise is a major issue. Some of the strategies to promote peace and harmony include:

- Disseminating information on non-violent resolutions of ethnic and communal conflicts in the Priorities 1 and 2 countries.
- Networking of NGOs, politicians, and other actors interested to promote peace at sub-regional and regional levels; and local peace committees in NGO field areas which are conflict-ridden.
- Strengthening gender-sensitivity of relief and rehabilitation efforts through training and dissemination of materials/kits.
- Strengthening women's representation in, and gender sensitivity of, the international and national peace keeping forces.
- Strengthening support services available for women with post-stress disorders, as well as soldiers.

Women's rights to just legislation and practices

Gender-just legislation and practices are *necessary* if women are to claim their rights in other spheres – be it rights to land, rights to equal wages, rights to political participation, rights to freedom from violence and so on. Ratification of international human rights instruments by member countries can also enhance the space available for women for legal redress. However, these measures are *not sufficient* by themselves to reduce poverty and promote women's human rights, and need to be combined by bottom-up strategies towards women's legal/human rights literacy and empowerment.

Though all countries require some degree of legal reform or the other, there is an urgent need for intervention in some. Afghanistan, Myanmar and Democratic People's Republic of Korea in Asia and Kazakhstan, Kyrgyzstan and Turkmenistan are yet to sign (except Afghanistan) or ratify the Convention on Elimination of Discrimination Against Women and hence there is need for international pressure. Further, there is also a need to put international pressure to remove reservations placed by some of the countries in Asia and the CIS on particular articles (especially in the realm of the family and religion), and to ratify the protocol of the Convention which allows women to submit complaints directly to the Committee. National Governments which have not ratified all other human rights instruments like the International Covenant on Economic, Social and Cultural Rights, International Covenant on Civil and Political Rights, Convention on the Rights of the Child and the Convention relating to the status of the refugees should be encouraged to do so immediately (see Chapter 4, Table 4.1).

Some of the other strategies required to promote women's rights to gender-just legislation and practices include:
- Strengthening mechanisms to monitor and report on adherence to the Convention by all member countries, especially in priority countries where women's movement is not active.

- Legal reform to ensure that customary or/religious laws which over-ride/co-exist with statutory law should be in compliance with international human rights norms, especially with regard to family and personal law.
- Disseminating information on women's legal rights and strengthening women's access to formal legal structures and informal systems of legal redress which are gender conscious.
- Strengthening efforts to carry out legal and human rights literacy programmes.
- Strengthening/advocating National Commissions for Women with independent powers, resources and personnel.

Regional Prioritisation of Issues: A summary

Almost every issue is important to address in all the countries, but some of them need an added emphasis in particular regions, sub-regions and countries:

- **In South Asia**, the issues of *promoting* women's land rights, female literacy and elementary education, women's participation in paid work with just wages, women's reproductive rights, women's political participation and women's rights to peace need an added emphasis. Women's rights to food security is an urgent issue in Sri Lanka, Bangladesh, Afghanistan and Pakistan.
- **In South-East Asian countries under transition and in China** the key issues include *protecting* women's land rights in the process of transition, protecting girl children's access to education, protecting women's employment and conditions of work, strengthening women's political participation and promoting the rights of sex workers. Women's rights to food security is particularly important in the PDR of Laos and China. In China and Vietnam there is an urgent need to protect marine resources and women's rights to the catch of fish. Rights of female infants and foetuses is an issue of specific relevance to China. The issue of maintaining peace and harmony is perhaps pressing in Cambodia and Myanmar, while in China the issue is strengthening democracy.

- In capitalist South-East Asian countries, the key issues include *protecting* girl children's education and women's employment in the light of the economic crisis, promoting equal wages for work of equal value, promoting women's rights to common property resources, promoting the rights of sex workers and migrant workers, and women's political participation. Women's right to food security is a major issue in Malaysia, Indonesia and the Philippines. In conflict-ridden Malaysia and Indonesia, the issues of restoring peace and democracy are important.
- In the CIS countries, the key issues in the light of transition to a market-led and democratic form of governance include protecting women's employment and education of girl children, protecting rural women's land rights, strengthening social security for the unemployed, elderly and single parents, protecting women's political participation, protecting the rights of refugees in the transition process, and promoting peace and harmony in conflict-ridden areas.

Some of these issues may require interventions more at the regional or sub-regional level (issues of gender and trade, trafficking and peace), while others may require more intra-country level interventions (gender and law, health/education, for e.g.). A majority of the issues, however, may require interventions at multiple levels (food security, work and employment, environment) and multiple institutional sites (households, community, market, state and international institutions). A more detailed analysis at the regional and country level,[12] as well as an assessment by the NGOs of its own internal strengths, are required to determine on which issues the NGO should intervene directly, and those on which existing efforts of government, aid agencies, other NGOs or the corporate sector should be strengthened.

Mapping of Regional Organisations Working on Emerging Issues

A preliminary review of the work being carried out by some of the regional non-governmental organisations in Asia suggest that there may be very few NGOs working wholistically on land rights, food security and common property resource management, education, and political participation and governance. Many organisations in the region seem to be working around the issues of trafficking of women for sexual and other purposes, gender, health and reproductive rights, gender, work and employment, and gender and human rights. Though there seems to be quite a few organisations working on gender issues in trade, most of them specialise in few areas linked to trade (like women in EPZs), and do not address the issue wholistically. On organisations working in the CIS region, a more indepth study is definitely warranted.

Emerging Areas for Research

Apart from throwing up some of the key issues which may need to be addressed in the coming decade, the analyses suggest several key areas where indepth studies/research may be required on the issue of gender and poverty and human rights violations:

- development of a data base and computation of human poverty index with specific reference to women in the region.
- gender and poverty across the CIS, in particular Moldova and Georgia, Afghanistan, Bhutan, and north-east part of Sri Lanka in South Asia and Myanmar in South-East Asia.
- indepth analysis of how some countries have achieved remarkable progress in the well-being of women at low levels of growth and per capita income.
- incidence of women headship and the vulnerability of different categories of WHH to poverty, and whether education disadvantage is passed on to the next generation to a greater extent than MHH.

- the gender and age composition of poor households vis-à-vis non-poor households.
- the implications of dispossession of land on women's poverty in transition economies.
- women's access to water for irrigation, and implications on their autonomy and well-being.
- possible strategies for expanding women's access to and participation in agricultural markets, and non-farm income generation possibilities for women especially in South Asia.
- the incidence and severity of poverty amongst unpaid women cultivators in small and marginal holdings of their husbands vs. landless labourers/women cultivating their own plots of land.
- gender-specific concerns of men in poverty arising out of social construction of masculinity.
- reasons for the sex ratio in Bhutan being significantly in favour of women.
- reasons for increase in suicide rates and domestic violence in Kerala, despite progress in human development, and low levels of gender disparity in education and health.

End Notes

1. Those directly affected by HIV/AIDS, and those in families affected by HIV/AIDS.
2. Including right to alternative employment.
3. Republic of Korea is another country whose GDP is significantly dependent on trade, but it is not included here as it is not a priority country.
4. Republic of Korea, Korea People's Democratic Republic and Malaysia are three other countries which are below or likely to cross the import dependency threshold by 2020, but they are not included here as they do not constitute priority countries.
5. Among Priorities 1 and 2 countries, China is yet to ratify equal pay for work of equal value. Hong Kong, Korea, Malaysia, Singapore and Thailand have also not ratified this clause.
6. For example, adherence to ILO Convention No. 100 on equal pay and compensation for women displaced by trade.
7. Especially in those Priorities 1 and 2 countries wherein AA is not working.

Chapter Six

Implications for Policy

The situational analysis on gender and poverty in Asia and the CIS suggests that not only does poverty persist in these two regions but also there is indeed a feminisation of poverty. Women and girl children in these two regions experience poverty in certain gender-specific ways and more intensely than men, and they face lesser options to overcome poverty. Poor women and girl children are also driven to adopt certain gender-specific coping strategies. It is therefore imperative that development agencies – government, multilateral aid agencies and non-governmental organisations – focus on poverty reduction of women and girl children in these two regions.

Strategies for Addressing Feminisation of Poverty

At the same time, merely focussing poverty reduction programmes on women and girl children is not enough, as poverty is experienced by these two groups in certain gender-specific ways, as well as ways specific to other social relations. Hence interventions to specifically address the gender-specific aspects of institutional exclusion in each sub-region, country or pocket may be required. For example, support for any relief programme in the South Asian countries would need to ensure that girl children and women eat in the distribution centre itself, rather than carry food to their homes or their temporary shelters, where male members of their households may consume it fully or deprive them of a large share. Merely opening schools for girl children may not be enough in most of the countries of Asia and the CIS. Instead, the gender-specific barriers to the education of girl children would have to be addressed.

The situational analysis revealed that poor women are also driven to adopt negative gender-specific coping strategies. Some examples of these are engaging in prostitution, illegal migration across borders, selling off their daughters for money, marrying off daughters when they are young, marrying off daughters to elderly persons and cutting down their own consumption of food and that of their daughters and so on. These negative coping strategies lead to gross violation of human rights of women and girl children. It is important to create an environment wherein women in poverty, their families, and their communities can abandon these negative coping strategies, and strengthen or adopt more positive ones. Grain banks, thrift and savings, collective purchase of consumption goods, collective sale of produce, and group health insurance managed by poor women's groups are few examples of such positive coping strategies

Nevertheless, these positive coping strategies of poor women would only temporarily mitigate poverty. There is hence a need for development agencies to address the gender-specific causes of women's poverty through expanding women's ownership entitlements, endowments, production possibilities and exchange options vis-à-vis different institutions of society. This demands that development agencies adopt an 'entitlements' or 'rights' perspective to address the gender-specific (and other social relations) causes of women's poverty. The assumption of international aid agencies and national governments that a less radical 'basic needs' or 'anti-poverty' approach is adequate for reducing women's poverty may not really hold good. A direct attack on basic needs (except education, which also has a high instrumental value and could be seen as extending exchange entitlement) may be appropriate only in emergency situations like drought, disasters, communal riots and so on. The exact points of structural intervention would vary from sub-region to sub-region (ref. Box, p 148). But transforming the kinship and inheritance systems in favour of women, promoting male responsibility for reproductive work, increasing women's representation and participation in public decision-making, and engendering the international and national legal system may be an essential pre-condition in most of the countries of Asia and the CIS.

The situational analysis suggests that the estimate that 70 per cent of the poor in Asia and the CIS are women is likely to be an exaggeration (even in South Asia). However, since the analysis of the impact of globalisation points to the high probability that both poverty levels and the proportion of women among the poor may increase in future. If the adverse effects of globalisation on women are to be contained, more importance should be given to address the causes than the manifestations, even in the short-run.

Priority Sub-regions, Countries and Groups for Poverty Reduction

Aid agencies may face the question as to which countries or sub-regions to focus upon within Asia and the CIS. As the absolute level of deprivation, the extent of feminisation of poverty, and the absolute numbers of women and girl children in poverty vary across different sub-regions and countries (and in different ways depending on which of the above three variables is emphasised), development agencies may need to decide what criteria they are going to adopt to prioritise geographical areas within Asia and the CIS for gender-specific intervention. If they take the absolute level of deprivation amongst women as the criteria for prioritising countries, first priority may need to be given to Nepal, Bangladesh, Pakistan, Bhutan, India, Cambodia, the PDR of Laos, Myanmar and parts of Vietnam. Though on Afghanistan there is very little information, it may also fall into this category. If the extent of feminisation of poverty was the criteria adopted, then South Asia would need maximum attention. However, if the absolute number of poor women is the criteria adopted, India and China merit the maximum attention. Ideally, striking a balance between the three criteria may be the best option.

Regional Prioritisation of Structural Interventions for Poverty Reduction

Key interventions required for poverty reduction include:

In **South Asia**: *promoting* women's land rights, female literacy and elementary education, women's participation in paid work with just wages, women's rights to natural resources, and intra-household equity in resource allocation. Household food security is a key issue all over the region, and national food security in Sri Lanka, Bangladesh, Afghanistan and Pakistan

In **South-East Asian countries under transition and in China**: *protecting* women's land rights, education, health, employment and political participation in the process of transition. Household food security is a key issue all over the region and national food security in the PDR of Laos and in China.

In **capitalist South-East Asian countries:**

protecting girl children's education and women's employment in the context of economic crisis, rights of migrant women and sex workers affected by economic crisis, promoting equal wages for work of equal value and promoting women's rights to common property resources. National food security is a major issue in Malaysia, Indonesia and the Philippines.

In **the CIS countries:**

protecting women's employment, education of girl children and women's land rights, strengthening social security for the unemployed, elderly and single parents. All this in the context of economic crisis and protecting women's political participation and protecting the rights of refugees in the process of political transition.

While absolute levels of poverty, extent of feminisation of poverty or numerical number of women and girl children may point to the necessity for focusing on South Asia, China and the Mekong parts of SE Asia, one cannot ignore the needs and concerns of poor women in the present medium/high human development countries of South-East Asia and the CIS most adversely affected by the process of economic crisis and transition. This includes Indonesia, the Philippines, Thailand and Malaysia in South-East Asia, and Kyrgyzstan, Tajikistan, Uzbekistan, Armenia, Georgia, Azerbaijan and Moldova in the CIS. In particular, safety net interventions – wage employment and social security measures – for women in Indonesia may be warranted, as the incidence of poverty is expected to double by the end of the century

The incidence of poverty among women and the extent of its feminisation also varies across ethnic, caste, class, age, marital status and so on, suggesting the need for development agencies specially focusing on women from ethnic minorities, dalits, landless labourers, bonded labourers, the urban informal sector, artisanal fishworkers, in environmental fragile zones, in human poverty from non-poor households, refugee women, girl children and the elderly and the disabled. Some groups may need more attention in some sub-regions than others. Depending on the prioritisation of sub-regions/countries, particular sections among WHHs households may also need to be focused upon.

Rethinking Present Debates on Gender and Poverty

Though not the central focus of this study, the analysis on gender, poverty and human rights in Asia and the CIS also throws light on the current debates on gender and poverty (whether gender issues should be confined to issues of poverty, and poverty issues with women). Underneath this debate is the assumption that human rights violations against women and poverty of women are two entirely separate issues. In reality, there is a significant overlap between the two. If one decides to take on board and address the gender-specific causes of poverty, many of the human rights violations against women (though not all) would also be addressed; thus pointing to a possible way of resolving some of the differences in viewpoints on the validity of the gender and poverty agenda.

However, the analysis suggests that equating 'gender and poverty' concerns exclusively with women can take attention away from gender-specific ways in which men get affected by poverty. The fact that mainly men committ suicide in Andhra Pradesh in India when faced with crop damage, that men are disadvantaged in the Philippines with respect to education, and that the education of boys suffered more in Mongolia due to the economic crisis, point to the need to address the gender-specific needs of men in poverty as well. It is time that development agencies paid attention to examining the relationship between gender, poverty and men.

Balancing Poverty Reduction with Human Rights Agenda

The chapter on analyses of human rights violations in the two regions suggests that there are several human rights violations against women *qua* women in the two regions, irrespective of their economic status. Hence the rights approach to development is important not just for arresting feminisation of poverty but also protecting and promoting the larger canvas of human rights of women. In this context development agencies may face the dilemma of how much weight to give to reducing women's poverty and how much to protecting and promoting human rights violations against women within its gender policy. A way of resolving this dilemma is to focus more on addressing the gender-specific causes of women's poverty and less on its manifestations. In the processes many of the human rights concerns of women *qua* women and poverty concerns of poor women (for example, equal wages, property rights, increasing women's political participation) would be simultaneously addressed. The human rights issues which may not be attended through such a process include freedom from violence against women, women's reproductive rights and male reproductive responsibility, rights of female foetuses to live, and women's rights to peace and harmony. These may require sub-regional and country level campaigns.

Several priority areas for action have been highlighted related to gender, poverty and human rights concerns in these two regions. Some issues need to be addressed all over, while others are specific to particular countries/sub-regions. Some issues may require interventions more at the regional or sub-regional level (issues of gender and trade, trafficking and peace), while others may require more intra-country level interventions (gender and law, health/ education, for e.g.). A majority of the issues, however, may require interventions at multiple levels (food security, work and employment and environment) and multiple institutional sites (households, community, market, state and international institutions). The challenge would be for development agencies to intervene strategically at different levels.

Annexure 1

Poverty amongst Women-Headed Household

Region/Country	Incidence of household headship	Proportion below the poverty line	Source
South-East Asia:			
PDR of Laos	15 per cent urban and 10 per cent of rural HH are WHH (ESCAP, 1998) 52 per cent of them are widows.	No rigorous empirical data. One micro study indicates that incidence and depth of poverty is lower among WHH than MHH.	ESCAP, 1998 cited in Esser, 1998. 1992–3 Lao Expenditure and Consumption Survey, cited in World Bank, 1996.
Cambodia	23 per cent of HH are WHH. (EAIHR, 1995) 26 per cent of all HH are WHH. 30 per cent urban, and 25 per cent rural. ESCAP (1998).	No empirical data. One study suggests that WHH in rural areas and widows are the most marginalised and vulnerable, although this may not be true for WHH on an average.	EAIHR (World Bank), 1995 cited in World Bank, 1996 ESCAP (1998) cited in Esser, 1998.
Vietnam	27 per cent of total households (Desai) 32 per cent of total households (ESCAP, 1998). 50 per cent in urban and 28 per cent in rural areas.	There is no simple association between women headship and poverty. WHH wherein the male spouse is working away from the HH are not poor, and in fact may be better off than the MHH. Single parent WHH are poor, but so are single parent MHH. However, single parent MHH are fewer in proportion.	Desai (1995) cited in World Bank, 1996, Mc Donald, 1995. ESCAP, 1998 cited in Esser, 1998. Poverty profile: Mc Donald (1995) ACTIONAID-Vietnam, 1997 Vietnam Living Standard Survey, (1993).[1]

[1] *Communicating with Ms Quann, ActionAid, Vietnam.*

Indonesia	14 per cent of total households (1987), a decline from 16 per cent in 1975.	NI	Bruce et al, 1995,[2] cited in Buvinic and Gupta.
Thailand	An increase from 12.5 per cent in 1975.	The proportion of poor households headed by women is roughly the same for non-poor.	Bruce et al, 1995, cited in Buvinic and Gupta, 1997. World Bank (1997b).
Philippines	11 per cent of all HH in 1990, more or less the same as in 1970.	45 per cent of WHH in poverty. The incidence and severity of poverty is significantly less in WHH as they tend to be absorbed into others.	World Bank (1997b).
East Asia Monmgolia	18 per cent of all HH are WHH.	Nearly 60 per cent of individuals living in WHH are poor, compared to 31 per cent in MHH.	EA2RS (World Bank), 1996 cited in World Bank, 1996.
China		NI	
Hong Kong	25.7 per cent of all HH (1991).	NI	Bruce et al, cited in Buvinic and Gupta 1997.
South Korea	15 per cent of all households.	NI	
South Asia Bangladesh	17 per cent of all households.	95 per cent fall below the poverty line. Their incomes are 40 per cent less than MHH amongst the extreme poor.	Bruce et al, cited in Buvinic and Gupta 1997. ACTIONAID-Bangladesh, 1998.
India	19–20 per cent of households in the 1970s (non-governmental estimation)	Widowed women in North India are poorer than married women of the same age, caste and class.	Buvinic and Youseff (1978) cited in Agarwal (1994) on the incidence of womenheadship.

[2] *Bruce et al (1995) use either demographic survey data or census data*

	10 per cent according to the 1991 national census.	Though widowed men are equally poor, the incidence of male widowhood is lower.[3] Upper-caste widowed/deserted women in South India with no male children and kinship support systems tend to be poorer than married women from the same caste.	National census figures also cited in Agarwal (1994). Chen and Dreze, 1995 on widows. Lingam, 1994.
Sri Lanka	18 per cent of all households in 1987, an increase from 16 per cent in 1975.	NI	Bruce et al, 1995.
CIS Kazakhstan	No estimate available	Unmarried mothers, and women with large families in rural areas amongst the poorest*	
Uzbekistan	No estimate available	Rural women with large families amongst the poorest.*	
Ukraine	No estimate available	Single mothers, and women with many children amongst the poorest*.	
Kyrgyzstan	No estimate available	Single mothers are amongst the poorest	Howell (1996 a and b)
Tajikistan	No estimate available	Women with large families. As rate of remarriage is higher.	

[3] As rate of remarriage is higher
* Not clear whether women with large families are heading their HH.

Annexure 2

Mapping of Regional organisations Working Around Specific Issues

Emerging Issues	South Asia/CIS level NGOs/Networks	South-East Asia/East Asia level NGOs/Networks
Women's Rights to Productive Resources	Centre for Women's Development Studies, New Delhi. Indian Institute for Economic Growth, New Delhi. Centre for Social Research, New Delhi. Women and Development Center, Baku, Azerbaijan.	Asia and Pacific Development Centre, (APDC) Kuala Lumpur. Gender and Development Research Institute, Thailand. Asia Pacific Social Development Resource Centre, Hong Kong. Asian Cultural Forum on Development, Thailand.
Women's Rights to Health, Education and Child Care:	Asian Community Health Action Network, ACHAN, India. Chetna, Ahemdabad. Indian Institute of Management, Bangalore. Asia South Pacific Bureau of Adult Education (ASPBEA), Mumbai. Institute of Development Studies, Jaipur. DAWN South Asia,	Asian Coalition for Housing Rights, Thailand Society for Women's Initiative Funds, Vietnam (Vietnam, PDR of Laos and Cambodia). Asia Pacific Resource and Research Centre for Women, Malaysia. Asian Health Institute, Japan. Asian Pacific Disability Rehabilitation Organisation. Asia South Pacific Bureau of Adult Education, Thailand. South-East Asia Regional Institute for Community Education, Philippines.

		Institute of South-East Asian Studies, Singapore. Kalyanamitra, Indonesia.
Women's Rights to Gender-just Trade, Capital Flows and Technology Flow	Trivandrum, India. UNIFEM, New Delhi. International Collective In Support of Fishworkers, Chennai, India. Public Interest Legal Support and Research Centre, New Delhi. Indian Institute of Management, Bangalore.	DAWN, South-East Asia, Philippines. UNIFEM, Bangkok. Consumer International Regional Office for Asia and the Pacific (CIROAP), Thailand. Asia Monitor Resource Centre, Hong Kong. Association for Women for Action and Research, Singapore. Focus on the Global South, Bangkok.
Women's Rights to Food Security	Centre for Women's Development Studies, New Delhi. FAO-Freedom from Hunger Campaign, New Delhi. International Collective in Support of Fishworkers.	Asian Institute of Technology, Bangkok. Jude Howell, School of Development Studies, University of East Anglia.
Women's Rights to Employment/ Wages/Rest	Akshara, Mumbai. Centre for Social Research, New Delhi. ICECD, Ahmedabad INFORM, Colombo.	Friends of Women Foundation, Thailand. Foundation for Women, Thailand Kharkiv Women's Resource Center, Kharkiv, Ukraine.
Women's Rights to CPRs/Natural Resource Management	Centre For Environment, Community Development and Gender, Nepal	ENGENDER, Singapore Pan Asia and the Pacific, Malaysia (pesticides). Asian Indigenous Women's Network, Philippines.

Annexure 2

	International Institute for Human Rights, Environment and Development (INHURED), Lalitpur, Nepal.	Asian Indigenous Women's Network, Philippines. Asian Institute of Technology, Bangkok.
	Institute of Rural Management, Anand.	
	Centre for Women's Development Studies, New Delhi.	
Women's Rights to Political Participation and Just Governance	ISST, Bangalore/ New Delhi, India. SEARCH, Bangalore, India. National Institute of Advanced Studies, Bangalore, India.	Centre for Asia Pacific Women in Politics, the Philippines. Organisation of Women Parliamentarians from Muslim countries.
Women's Reproductive Rights	Jagori, New Delhi. Voluntary Health Association of India, New Delhi.	ARROW, Malaysia.
Women's Rights to Freedom from Violence	Radhika Coomaraswamy, Colombo (Special Rappoteur–violence against women). Asian Women's Human Rights Commission, Bangalore. War Against Rape, Karachi. Badari, Pakistan. Women and Media Collective, Colombo. Centre for Women's Research (CENWOR), Colombo. Jagori, New Delhi. Vimochana, Bangalore.	Asian Human Rights Commission, Hong Kong. Association of Women of Asia and the Pacific, Singapore. Asian Legal Resource Centre, Hong Kong. Amnesty International, Asia Pacific Regional Office, Hong Kong. Friends of Women Foundation, Thailand.

Rights of Sex Workers:	Asian Women's Human Rights Commission, Bangalore.	Human's Rights Watch, Asia and the Pacific.
		Global Alliance Against Trafficked Women, Thailand/Netherlands.
		International Organization for Migration, Bangkok.
		Coalition Against Traffic in Women, the Philippines.
		International Movement Against All Forms of Discrimination and Racism, Japan.
		Asian Human Rights Commission, Hong Kong.
		Asian Legal Resource Centre, Hong Kong.
Women's Rights to Peace and Harmony:	Tibetan Women's Association, Himachal Pradesh.	Women's Federation for World Peace, the Philippines.
	National Alliance of Women, New Delhi.	Network Women's Programme OSI, New York (working with CIS countries).
	Indian Social Institute, New Delhi.	
	Sulh Women's Society, Azerbaijan.	
Women's Rights to Just Legal System	Asian Women's Human Rights Commission.	International Women's Rights Action Watch, Kuala Lumpur.
	INHURED, Lalitpur, Nepal.	Asian Pacific Women Law and Development, Bangkok.
	South Asia Forum for Human Rights, Kathmandu, Nepal.	
	Nari-Pokko, Bangladesh.	Asian Human Rights Commission, Hong Kong.
	Women and Media Collective, Colombo.	
	CENWOR, Colombo.	Asian Regional Resource Centre for Human Rights Education, Thailand.

| | Azerbaijan Gadin Huguglary Mudafisy, Baku. | Asian Legal Resource Centre, Hong Kong. Women's Watch – Asia and Pacific Chapter. Asian Centre For Women's Human Rights, the Philippines. Kalyanamitra, Jakarta. (only Indonesia). |

Glossary

A
- *ani-ani* — simple blade tool used by women traditionally for harvesting
- APEC — Asian Pacific Economic Cooperation
- ASEAN — Association of South-East Asian Nations

B
- *bancas* — motorised fishing boats
- *bawon* — Indonesian system of universal participation in harvesting operations
- BIMARU belt — comprising the States of Bihar, Orissa, Madhya Pradesh, Rajasthan and Uttar Pradesh
- BPL — below the poverty line

C
- *ceblokon* — system wherein payments are made in cash
- CEDAW — Committee on the Elimination of all forms of Discrimination Against Women
- CIS — Commonwealth of Independent States include Kazakhstan, Kyrgyzstan, Uzbekistan, Tajikistan and Turkmenistan belonging to the Central Asian sub-region, Armenia, Azerbaijan and Georgia belonging to the Transcaucasus sub-region and Russia, Belarus, Ukraine and Moldova
- CPRs — Common Property Resources

E
- EPZ — Export procesing zone

F
- FHH — Female headed households

G
- GAATW — Global Alliance Against Trafficking in Women
- GEM — Gender empowerment measure
- GDI — Gender-related development index

H
- HDI — Human development index
- HDR — Human Development Report
- HPI — Human poverty index

M
- MHH — Male headed household
- MMR — Maternal Mortality Rate
- MNCs — Multinational(s) Companies

R
- RGWG — Regional Gender Working Group

S
- SAARC — South Asian Alliance for Regional Countries

T
- TNC — Transnational Corporation
- TRIPS — Trade Related Intellectual Property Rights

U
- UNHCR — United Nations High Commission for Refugees
- USSR — Union of Soviet Socialist Russia

W
- WTO — World Trade Organisation

Bibliography

A

Achan, 1995, 'In Focus-Cambodia and Quiet Flows the Mekong?', in *Link Vol. 13, No.2.*

ACTIONAID- Pakistan, 1997, *Gender and Poverty in Pakistan: A Background Paper*, ACTIONAID, Islamabad.

ACTIONAID-Bangladesh,1994, *ACTIONAID Bangladesh Country Strategy Paper 1994–1998*, ACTIONAID, Dhaka.

ACTIONAID-Nepal, *Gender Status Report for Regional Workshop on Gender*, ACTIONAID, Bangalore.

ACTIONAID-Nepal, 1994, *Strategy Paper 1994-1998*, ACTIONAID, Kathmandu.

ACTIONAID-Vietnam, 1997, *ACTIONAID Vietnam Country Strategy Paper: 1997–2000*, ACTIONAID, Hanoi.

Agnihotri, S B, 1995, *Missing Females: A Disaggregated Analysis, Vol. XXX No. 33.*

Asian Development Bank, 1995a, *Women in Development: Vietnam*, Programs Department (West), Asian Development Bank, Bangkok.

Asian Development Bank, 1995b, *Women in Development: Mongolia*, Programs Department East, Asian Development Bank, Bangkok.

Asian Development Bank, 1996a, *Women in Development: Cambodia*, Programs Department (West), Asian Development Bank, Bangkok.

Asian Development Bank, 1996b, *Women in Development: Lao PDR*, Programs Department West and Social Development Division, Asian Development Bank, Bangkok.

Asian Development Bank, 1998, *Asian Development Outlook*, Oxford University Press, New York.

Afghan Mission, 1998, *Summary of the Report of the Gender Mission to Afghanistan, Jan 1998*, UNHCR, Switzerland.

Afsharipur, A, 1997, *Expert Group Meeting on State Interventions on Violence Against Women 14-18 June*, organised by Ministry of Women and Children Affairs, Government of Bangladesh.

Agarwal, B, 1994, *A Field of One's Own: Gender and Land Rights in South Asia*, Cambridge University Press, New York, USA.

Agarwal, B, 1997, 'Bargaining and Gender Relations Within and Beyond the Household', in *Feminist Economics, Vol. 3 No. 1.*

Ahmed, I (Ed.), 1985, *Technology and Rural Women: Conceptual and Empirical Issues*, George Allen and UNWIN, London.

Ahmed, S, 1998a, 'Rural Women and the Environment: Shared Concerns?', in *IRMA Working Paper 49.*

Ahmed, S, 1998b, 'Women's Role in Natural Resources Management', in *Women in the Third World – An Encyclopedia of Contemporary Issues.*

Ahmed, S and Krishna, N H, 1998, 'Changing Gender Roles in Irrigation Management: The Case of Sadguru's Lift-Irrigation Co-Operatives', in *IRMA Working Paper 120.*

Ahn, Y, 1996, 'Out Of The Darkness: The Story of a 'Comfort Woman'', in *Indian Journal of Gender Studies*, Sage Publications, New Delhi.

AIDSCAP, 1997, 'Status and Trends of HIV/AIDS Epidemics in Asia and the Pacific: A Provisional Report', AIDSCAP, Manila.

ARROW, 1998, *ARROWS for Change, Vol. 4 No. 2*, ARROW, Kuala Lampur.

B

Banerjee, N, 1997, 'How Real is the Bogey of Feminization?', in *The Indian Journal of Labour Economics, Vol. 40, No.3.*

Bardhan, K, 1993, 'Women and Rural Poverty: Some Asian Cases', in *Rural Poverty in Asia: Priority Issues and Policy Options,* Asian Development Bank, Manila.

Barrett, G, and Versak, K, 1998, on 'Everyone's Miracle? Revisiting Poverty and Inequality in East Asia', in The World Bank, Press Release.

Baulch, B, 1996, 'The New Poverty Agenda: A Disputed Consensus', in *IDS Bulletin, Vol. 27 No.1.*

Beall, J, 1996, 'Participation in the City: Where do Women Fit in?', in *Gender and Development Vol. 4 No.1.*

Begum, R, 1993, 'Women in Environmental Disasters: The 1991 Cyclone in Bangladesh', in *Focus on Gender, Vol. 1 No.1.*

Bello, W, 1997, 'Neither Market Nor State: The Development Debate in South-East Asia', in *The Ecologist Asia, Vol. 5 No.5.*

Bhargava, K K, Bongartz, H, and Sobhan, F, 1995, *Shaping South Asia's Future-Role of Regional Cooperation,* Vikas Publishing House Pvt. Ltd., New Delhi.

Bhatia, A, 1997, 'Power, Equity, Gender, and Conflicts in Common Property Resources in the Hindu Kush-Himalayas', in *Issues in Mountain Development 97/7.*

Bhatta, P, Neupane, S, Thapa, S, Baker, J, and Friedman, M, 1993, *Commercial Sex Workers in Kathmandu Valley -Their Profile and Health Status,* AIDS and STDs Prevention Network Valley Research Group, Kathmandu, Nepal.

Bhattacharya, B, and Rani, G J, 1995, 'Gender In Agriculture: An Asian Perspective', in *Asia-Pacific Journal of Rural Development, Vol. V No.1,* Somporn Hanpongpandh, Bangladesh.

Binh, D T, 1997, 'Some Problems Concerning Social Policies Towards Vietnamese Rural Women in the Market Economy', in *Asia Pacific Forum on Women, Law and Development, Vol. 10, No.2.*

Blanc-Szanton, M C, 1990, 'Gender and Inter-Generational Resource Allocation Among Thai and Sino-Thai Households', in Dube and Palriwala (Eds.), *Structures and Strategies: Women, Work and Family,* SAGE Publications, New Delhi.

Bloom, G, and Xingyuan, G, 1997, 'Introduction to Health Sector Reform in China', in *IDS Bulletin, Vol 28 No.1.*

Brakel, and Anderson, 1998, 'Socio-Economic Status of Women with Disabilities in an Urban Community in China', in *Asia Pacific Disability Rehabilitation Journal, Vol. 9 No.2.*

Braun, J V, 1995, 'Employment for Poverty Reduction and Food Security: Concept, Research Issues, and Overview', in International Food Policy Research Institute (Ed.), *Employment for Poverty Reduction and Food Security,* International Food Policy Research Institute, USA.

Brooks, K, Krylatykh, E, Lerman, Z, Petrikov, A, and Uzun, V, 1996, 'Agricultural Reform in Russia - A View from the Farm Level'- *World Bank Discussion Paper No.270,* World Bank, Washington DC.

Brown, L, 1997, 'Facing the Prospect of Food Scarcity' in Brown et al (Eds.) *State of The World 1997,* W W Norton and Company, New York and Earthworm Books, Chennai.

Buringa, J, Anmd L, Tshering, 1992, *Education and Gender in Bhutan: A Tentative Analysis,* National Women's Association of Bhutan.

Bushra, J E, and Mukarubuga, C, 1995, 'Women, War and Transition', in *Gender and Development, Vol. 3 No.3.*

Buvinic, M, and Gupta, G R, 1997, *Female-Headed Households and Female-Maintained Families: Are they Worth Targeting to Reduce Poverty in Developing Countries?,* International Centre for Research on Women and the Population Council, Washington.

C

Carlson, B A, 1994, 'The Condition of Children in the Countries of the Former Soviet Union (FSU): A Statistical Review', in *The Journal of Development Studies, Vol. 31 No.1.*

Chamberlain, S, 1996, 'World Trade is a Women's Issue: Report of a Conference 20–21 April, 1996', in *Focus on Gender Vol. 4 No.3.*

Chambers, R, 1988, *Putting The Last First,* Longman Scientific and Technical, New York.

Chen, M and Dreze, J, 1995, 'Social Security for Widows in India: Workshop and Conference Report', *Economic and Political Weekly, Vol. XXX No. 39.*

Clark, A W, 1995, *Gender and Political Economy-Explorations of South Asian Systems,* Oxford India Paperbacks.

Commins, S and A, Whaites, 1998, *Who will Bail the Poor? The Impact of the Asian Economic Crisis,* Paper Delivered at the Secretary of State for International Development's East Asian Seminar, London, July 15th, 1998

Consumers International Regional Office for Asia and Pacific, 1998, Thailand.

Cook, R J, 1996, 'Advancing Reproductive Rights Beyond Cairo and Beijing', in *Internal Family Planning Perspectives Vol. 22 No.3.*

Cottingham, S, Metcalf, K, and Phnuyal, B, 1998, 'The Reflect Approach to Literacy and Social Change: A Gender Perspective', in *Gender and Development, Vol. 6 No.2.*

Cox, T, and Suvedi, B K, 1994, *Sexual Networking in Five Urban Areas in the Nepal Terai,* AIDS and STDs Prevention Network Valley Research Group Kathmandu, Nepal.

Cukier, J, Norris, J, and Wall, G, 1996, 'The Involvement of Women in the Tourism Industry of Bali, Indonesia', in *The Journal of Development Studies, Vol. 33 No.2.*

Custers, P, 1997, *Capital Accumulation and Women's Labour in Asian Economies,* Vistaar Publications, New Delhi.

D

Dairiam, S, 1993, *Overview of Selected Strategies Related to some Forms of Violence Against Women,* International Women's Rights Action Watch, Malaysia

Davin, D, 1996, 'Gender and Rural-Urban Migration In China', in *Gender and Development, Vol. 4 No. 1.*

Davis and Klein, 1997, 'Gender, Culture and the Sea: Contemporary Theoretical Approaches', in Sachs (ed.) *Women Working in the Environment,* Taylor and Francis, USA. hj

Do Thi Binh and Le Ngoc Lan, 1997, *Poor Rural Women Under Market Economy,* Hanoi.

Dreze, J and A, Sen (Eds.), 1996, *Indian Development: Selected Regional Perspectives,* Oxford University Press, New Delhi.

Dube, L, 1997, *Women and Kinship: Comparative Perspectives on Gender in South and South-East Asia,* Visthaar Publications, New Delhi.

Dyson, T, and M, Moore, 1983, 'On Kinship Structure, Female Autonomy and Demographic Behaviour in India', in *Population and Development Review, 9 (1).*

E

Elson, D, 1991, 'Male Bias In Macro-Economic: The Case of Structural Adjustment', in D Elson (Ed.) *Male Bias in Development Process,* Manchester University Press, Manchester.

Emmott, S, 1996, 'Dislocation, Shelter and Crisis: Afghanistan's Refugees and Notions of Home', in *Gender and Development, Vol. 4 No.1.*

F

FAO, 1995, 'Issues in Rural Poverty, Employment and Food Security', in *World Summit for Social Development,* Copenhagen 6–12 May, FAO, Rome.

Fernando, N, 1997, *Trafficking in Asia – An Overview, Asian Human Rights Commission,* Bangkok.

Filmer, D, E M, King and L, Pritchett, 1998, 'Gender Disparity In South-Asia: Comparison Between and Within Countries', *Policy Research Working Paper, 1867,* The World Bank, Washington.

Floro, M S, 1994, 'The Dynamics of Economic Change and Gender Roles: Export Cropping in the Philippines', in *Mortgaging Women's Lives: Feminist Critique on Structural Adjustment,* United Nations, NewYork.

G

Gangoli, G, 1996, 'The Right to Protection from Sexual Assault: The Indian Anti-Rape Campaign', in *Development in Practice, Vol.6 No.4.*

Gardner, G, 1997, 'Preserving Global Cropland', in Brown et al (Eds.) *State of the World 1997,* W W Norton and Company, NewYork and Earthworm Books, Chennai.

Gathia, J, 1998, 'Child Labour in South Asia', in *Women's Link, Jan–March.*

Gandhi and Shah, 1991, *The Issues at Stake: Theory and Practice in the Contemporary Women's Movement in India,* Kali for Women, New Delhi.

GAATW, IOM and CWDA, 1997, Two Reports on the Situation of Women and Children Trafficked from Cambodia and Vietnam to Thailand, Global Alliance Against Trafficking of Women (GAATW), International Organisation for Migration (IOM) and Cambodian Women's Development Association (CWDA).

Goetz, A M, 1995, 'Institutionalising Women's Interests and Accountability to Women in Development', in *IDS Bulletin, Vol. 26 No. 3.*

Gotheskar, S, 1997, 'Women, Work And Health: An Interconnected Web- Case of Drugs and Cosmetics Industries', in *Economic and Political Weekly Vol. XXXII No.43,* Oct 25–31.

Government of Lao People's Democratic Republic, 1996, 'Practitioners' Papers-Food Security In Lao People's Democratic Republic: An Assessment of the Prevailing Situation and the Government's Food Security Regime', in *Asia-Pacific Journal of Rural Development Vol. VII No.1.*

Gurung, J D, 1995, *Agricultural Technologies Selected by Farm Women in Nepal,* International Centre for Integrated Mountain Development Kathmandu, Nepal.

Guzman, J S D, 1996, 'Trafficking of Filipino Women Migrants: A Product of Commodification of Women', in *Forum News, Vol. 9 No.3.*

H

Haan, A D, and Maxwell, S, 1998, 'Poverty and Social Exclusion in North and South', in *IDS Bulletin,*
Vol. 29 No.1.

Hale, A, 1996, 'The Deregulated Global Economy: Women Workers and Strategies of Resistance', *Focus on Gender, Vol. 4 No. 3.*

Haque, T, 1998, 'Issues Concerning Employment of Women in South Asia', in Labour, Employment and Human Development in South Asia, Institute for Human Development.

Harwin, J, and Fajth, G, 1998, 'Child Poverty and Social Exclusion in Post Communist Societies', in *IDS Bulletin , Vol. 29 No.1.*

Heeks, 1998, 'Flying Software: Is the Information Society Heading South', in *Insights, Issue 25.*

Heerden, A V, 1998, *Heyday for Free Zones. But will they last?,* International Labour Office, Switzerland.

Bibliography

Heyzer, N, 1992, *Gender Issues in Anti-Poverty Programs in Asia: Experiences And Issues*, The Economic Development Institute, The World Bank, Washington.

Heyzer, N, 1993, 'Gender, Economic Growth and Poverty', in *Focus on Gender, Vol. 1 No.3*.

Heyzer, N and V, Wee, 1992, 'Domestic Workers in Transient Overseas Employment: Who Benefits, Who Profits', in Heyzer et al (eds.) *The Trade in Domestic Workers: Causes, Mechanisms and Consequences of International Migration*, APDC, Kuala Lumpur.

Howell, J, 1995, 'Prospects for NGOs in China', in *Development in Practice, Vol. 5 No.1*.

Howell, J, 1996a, 'Coping with Transition: Insights from Kyrgyzstan', in *Third World Quarterly, Vol. 17 No.1*.

Howell, J, 1996b, 'Poverty and Transition in Kyrgyzstan: How some Households Cope', in *Central Asian Survey*.

Human Rights Watch, 1998, Global Report on Women's Human Rights, Oxford University Press, New York.

I

International Centre for Research on Women, 1998, Domestic Violence in India: Information Bulletin, PROWID, ICRW, Washington.

International Collective in Support of Fishworkers, 1996, Dossier Women in Fisheries No. 3, ICSF, Chennai

International Collective in Support of Fishworkers, 1997, Dossier Women in Fisheries No. 4, ICSF, Chennai

IDS BRIDGE, 'Development and Gender' in Brief 4, *Integrating Gender Into Emergency Responses*.

IFAD, 1995a, *The State of World Rural Poverty: A Profile of Asia*, IFAD, Rome.

IFAD, 1995b, *Conference on Hunger and Poverty: An Overview*, IFAD, Rome.

International Organisation for Migration, 1997, *Trafficking in Migrant Women and Children-IOM Responses to Date and Future Activities*, International Organisation for Migration, Bangkok

Ireson, C, 1997, 'Women's Forest Work In Laos', in Sachs., (Ed.) *Women Working in the Environment*, Taylor and Francis, USA.

Illo, J F, 1992, 'Who Heads the Household? Women in Households in the Philippines', in Saradamoni (Ed.), *Finding the Household: Conceptual and Methodological Issues*, SAGE, New Delhi.

J

Jackson, C, 1995, 'Rescuing Gender From The Poverty Trap', Gender Analysis in *Development Series,*
No. 10, University of East Anglia of Development Studies, Norwich.

Jafri, S M Y, and Raishad, 1997, 'Some Dimensions of Child Labour', in *The Pakistan Development Review*.

Jahan, R, 1998, 'Hidden Wounds, Visible Scars: Violence Against Women in Bangladesh', in Agarwal (Ed.), *Structures of Patriarchy*, Kali for Women, New Delhi.

Jianghui, L, Suhua, C, and Lucas, H, 1997, 'Utilisation of Health Services in Poor Rural China: An Analysis Using A Logistic Regression Model', in *IDS Bulletin, Vol. 28 No.1*.

Joekes, S, and Weston, A, 1994, *Women and the New Trade Agenda*, UNIFEM, New York.

Joekes, S, 1995, 'Gender and Livelihoods in Northern Pakistan', in *IDS Bulletin, Vol. 26 No. 1*.

Johnson, R, 1997, 'The Tobin Tax: Another Lost Opportunity?', in *Development in Practice, Vol. 7 No.2*.

Jun, L, and Xiaojiang, L, 1998, 'Women In China', in *Women in the Third World-an Encyclopedia of Contemporary Issues*.

K

Kabeer, N, 1994a, 'Reversed Realities: Gender Hierarchies', in *Development Thought*, Verso, London/New York.

Kabeer, N, 1994b, 'Gender-Aware Policy and Planning: A Social Relations Perspective', in Macdonald M (Ed.), *Gender Planning in Development Agencies: Meeting the Challenges*, Oxfam, United Kingdom.

Kabeer, N, 1997, 'Tactics and Trade-Offs: Revisiting the Links between Gender and Poverty', in *IDS Bulletin, Vol. 28 No.3*.

Kabir, M, 1998, 'Population Stabilization in Bangladesh', in *South Asia Green File, Vol. 3 No.10*.

Kapur, N, and Singh, K, 1993, *Practising Feminist Law – Some Reflections*, Paper Presented at Indian Association of Women's Studies Conference in 1993, Mysore.

Kapur, R, 1997, 'Women's Human Rights: A Critical Evaluation', in *Asia Pacific Forum on Women, Law and Development, Vol. 10 No.2*.

Kaufman, J, Kaining, Z, and Jing, F, 1997, 'Reproductive Health Financing, Service Availability and Needs in Rural China', in *IDS Bulletin, Vol. 28 No.1*.

Kazi, S, 1995, 'Rural Women, Poverty and Development in Pakistan', in *Asia Pacific Journal of Rural Development, Vol. V No.1*.

Kelkar, G, and Yunxian, W, 1997, 'Notes from the Field Farmers, Women and Economic Reform in China', in *Bulletin of Concerned Asian Scholars, Vol. 29 No.4*.

Khan, N A, and Begum, S A, 1997, 'Participation in Social Forestry Re-Examined: A Case-Study from Bangladesh', in *Development in Practice, Vol. 7 No.3*.

Khan, S A, 1998, Central Asia Sub-Region Situational Analysis, ACTIONAID, Pakistan.

Khor, M, 1996, 'The WTO and Foreign Investment: Implications and Alternatives for Developing Countries', in *Development in Practice, Vol. 6 No.4*.

Kolstee, T, Bijlmer, J, and Oosterhout, FV, 1994, *Urban Poverty Alleviation*, Ministry of Foreign Affairs, Netherlands.

Krishnaraj, M, Sudarshan, R M, and Shariff, A (Eds.), 1998, *Gender, Population and Development*, Oxford University Press, New Delhi.

Kyi, A S S, 1995, *Freedom from Fear and Other Writings*, Penguin Books, England.

L

Lakshmi, L, 1994, 'Women-Headed Households: Coping with Caste, Class and Gender Hierarchies', *Economic and Political Weekly, Vol. XXIX No. 12*.

Lansky, M, 1997, 'Perspectives-Child Labour: How the Challenge is being Met', in *International Labour Review, Vol. 136 No.2*.

Leach, M, Joekes, S, and Green, C, 1995, 'Editorial: Gender Relations and Environmental Change', in *IDS Bulletin, Vol. 26 No.1*.

Leach, F, 1996, 'Women in the Informal Sector: the Contribution of Education and Training', in *Development In Practice, Vol. 6 No.1*.

Lerman, Z, Brooks, K, and Csaki, C, 1994, 'Land Reform and Farm Restructuring in Ukraine' - *World Bank Discussion Paper No.270*, World Bank, Washington DC.

Lilly, F, 1997, *ACTIONAID and GAD: A History of the Corporate Effort up to 1996*, ACTIONAID Pakistan, Islamabad.

LINKS, 1997, *The Human Side of Conflict*, OXFAM, UK/Ireland

Lizee, P P, 1996, 'Cambodia in 1995: from Hope to Despair', in *Asia Survey, Vol. XXXVI, No 1*.

Lockwood, M and S, Baden, 1995, 'Beyond the Feminisation of Poverty: Gender-Aware Poverty Reduction', in *Bridge Development and Gender Brief, No. 2: Poverty Reduction Strategies*

Longwe, S H, 1997, 'The Evaporation of Gender Policies in the Patriarchal Cooking Pot', in *Development and Practice, Vol. 7 No.2.*

Longwe, S H, 1998, 'Education for Women's Empowerment or Schooling for Women's Subordination', in *Gender and Development, Vol. 6 No.2.*

Lou, J, 1997, 'Macroeconomic Reform in China – Laying The Foundation for a Socialist Market Economy', *World Bank Discussion Paper No.374*, The World Bank, Washington DC.

M

Macdonald, M, 1997, *Advocacy for Gender Sensitivity and Gender Equality in Development Corporation and Development Agencies*, Eurostep Publishers, Belgium.

Mahmud, D, 1997, 'Women's Work in Urban Bangladesh: Is there an Economic Rationale?', in *Development and Change, Vol. 28.*

Marcoux, A, 1998, 'The Feminization of Poverty: Claims, Facts, and Data Needs', in *Population and Development Review, Vol. 24 No.1.*

Martinez, L M, 1996, 'Recovering the Future: Grandmothers Campaigning for Human Rights', in *Development in Practice, Vol. 6 No.4.*

Mason, A D, 1996, 'Targeting the Poor in Rural Java', in *IDS Bulletin Vol. 27 No.1.*

Mathema, M, 1998, 'Women in South Asia: Pakistan, Bangladesh and Nepal', in *Women in the Third World: An Encyclopedia of Contemporary Issues.*

Mccall, M, 1996, 'Rural Brewing, Exclusion and Development Policy- Making', in *Gender and Development, Vol. 4 No.3.*

Mehmet, O, 1997, 'Development in a War-torn Society: What Next in Cambodia?', in *Third World Quarterly, Vol. 18 No.4.*

Mehra, R, Bruns, D, Carlson, P, Gupta, G R, and Lycette, M, 1995, *Engendering Development in Asia and the Near East: A Sourcebook*, ICRW, Washington DC.

Mehta, M, 1993, *Gender Dimensions of Poverty in Cambodia: A Survey Report*, Oxfam, Phnom Penh.

Meng, X, 1996, 'The Economic Position of Women in Asia', in *Asian-Pacific Economic Literature, Vol. 10 No.1.*

Mies, M, 1996, *Women, Food and Global Trade*, Institute Fur Theorie Und Praxis Der Subsistenz EV, Bielefeld.

Molyneux, M, 1995, 'Gendered Transitions: A Review Essay', in *Gender and Development, Vol. 3 No.3.*

Moon, G, 1995, *Free Trade: What's in it for Women, Background Report 6*, Community Aid Abroad, Melbourne.

Mukherjee, A, 1997, *The Many Faces of Global Poverty as We Move into the 21st Century*, ACTIONAID, Bangalore.

–, 1998, *A Proposal for ACTIONAID Interventions in China*, mimeo, ACTIONAID, Bangalore

Mukhopadhyay, S, and Savithri, R, 1998, *Poverty, Gender and Reproductive Choice – an Analysis of Linkages*, Manohar Publishers, New Delhi.

Murshid, K A S, 1998, 'Food Security – The Cambodian Experience: Poverty Emerging Challenges', Paper Presented at the International Conference on *Poverty Emerging Challenges* Organised by the Bangladesh Institute of Development Studies Held on 9–11th February, Dhaka, Bangladesh.

Murthi, M, A C, Guio and J, Dreze, 1996, 'Mortality, Fertility and Gender Bias in India: A District-Level Analysis', in Dreze, J Amd A K, Sen (Eds.), *Indian Development: Selected Regional Perspectives*, Oxford University Press, New Delhi.

Murthy, R K, 1996,'Fighting Female Infanticide by Working with Midwives: An Indian Case Study', in *Gender and Development, Vol. 4 No.2*.

Murthy, R, K, and Rao, N, 1997, *Addressing Poverty: Indian NGOs and Their Capacity Enhancement in the 1990s*, Friedrich Ebert Stiftung, New Delhi.

N

Nanavaty, R, 1997,'Feminise Our Forests: Consultation on The World Commission on Forests and Sustainable Development', in *Development in Practice, Vol. 7 No.4*.

Nepal South Asia Centre, 1998, *Nepal Human Development Report*, Nepal South Asia Centre, Nepal.

Nepal NGO Committee, 1996, *Food Security in Nepal: A Perspective of Non-Governmental Organisations*, ACTCOM, Nepal.

Nepal South Asia Centre, 1998, *Nepal Human Development Report*, Nepal.

Network of East-West Women, 1998a, *Report on the Legal Status of Women in Armenia*, Network of East-West Women East-East Legal Coalition, Network of East-West Women, Washington.

–, 1998b, *Report on The Legal Status of Women in Kyrgyz Republic*, Network of East-West Women East-East Legal Coalition, Washington.

Ngidang, D, 1995,'The Politics of Development in Longhouse Communities in Sarawak, East Malaysia', in *Development in Practice, Vol. 5 No.4*.

O

Oldenburg, P, 1992,'Sex Ratio, Son-Preference and Violence in India: A Research Note', *Economic and Politcial Weekly, Vol. XXVII Nos 49 & 50*.

Oliver, A, 1996,'Child-Care and The Benefits Trap: A Case from the UK', in *Gender and Development, Vol. 4 No.2*.

Oliveros, T, 1997,'Impact of World Trade on Peasant Women in the Philippines', in *Asia Pacific Forum on Women, Law and Development, Vol. 10 No.2*.

Omvedt, G, 1997,'Rural Women and The Family in an Era of Liberalization: India in Comparative Asian Perspective', in *Bulletin of Concerned Asian Scholars, Vol. 29 No.4*.

Oxfam, 1997, *Globalisation of the Economy: Gendered Impact on East/Southeast Asia Region*, Oxfam, Philippines.

P

Pairaudeau, N, and Minh Thu, N, 1996, *If I Had A Husband I Would Have A Better House*, A Study of Women – Headed Households in My Loc and Nhan Loc Communes, Can Loc District, Ha Tinh Province, Vietnam, ACTIONAID-Vietnam, Hanoi.

Patel, I, 1998, *Representation of Women in Mass Media Working Paper 95*, Institute for Rural Management, Anand, India.

Patel, I, 1998, *Women's Movement and Women's Education in India, Working Paper 116*, Institute for Rural Management Anand, India.

Petras, J, and Vieux, S, 1995,'Russia: The Transition to Underdevelopment', in *Journal of Contemporary Asia, Vol. 25 No.1*.

Pettman, J J, 1997,'Body Politics: International Sex Tourism', in *Third World Quarterly, Vol. 18, No.1*.

Pickup, F, 1998,'More Words But No Action? Forced Migration and Trafficking of Women', in *Gender and Development, Vol. 6 No.1*.

Bibliography

Pollock, J, 1996, 'Migration and Health: The Case of Illegal Female Migrants from Burma to Thailand', in *Forum News, Vol. 9 No.3.*

Poudel, M, and Shrestha, A, 1996, 'Dealing With Hidden Issues: Trafficked Women in Nepal', in *Development in Practice, Vol. 6 No.4.*

Phongpaichit, P, 1988, 'Two Roads to the Factory: Industrialisation Strategies and Women's Employment in South-East Asia', in Agarwal, B, (Ed.), *Structures of Patriarchy: State, Community and Household in Modernising Asia*, Kali For Women, New Delhi.

Prabhu, K S, P C, Sarkar and A Radha, 1996, in Rao, et al (Eds.), 'Gender-Related Development Index for Indian States: A Preliminary Exercise', in *Sites of Change: The Structural Context for Empowering Women in India*, Friedrich Ebert Stiftung, New Delhi.

Pradhan, M, and Prescott, N, 1997, *A Poverty Profile of Cambodia: World Bank Discussion Paper No. 373*, World Bank, Washington DC.

Prescott, N, 1997, *Poverty, Social Services, and Safety Nets in Vietnam*, World Bank Discussion Paper No.376, World Bank, Washington DC.

Q

Quy, L T, 1996, 'The Struggle against the Traffick in Women and Children in Vietnam', in *Forum News, Vol. 9 No.3.*

R

Rahman, H Z, 1998, 'Bangladesh: Dynamics of Rural Poverty', Paper Issued at The International Conference on *Poverty: Emerging Challenges* Organised by The Bangladesh Institute of Development Studies Held on 9-11th February, Dhaka, Bangladesh.

Rajan, I S, U S, Mishra and K, Navaneetham, 1992, Decline in Sex Ratio: Alternative Explanation Revisited, *Economic and Political Weekly, Vol. XXVII No. 46.*

Rakodi, C, 1996, 'Women in the City of Man: Recent Contributions to the Gender and Human Settlements Debate', in *Gender and Development, Vol. 4 No.1.*

Ramachandran, V (ed.), 1998, *Bridging the Gap between Intention and Action: Girls' and Women's Education in South Asia*, ASPBEA, New Delhi.

Ramanathan, M, 1997, 'Women in China – Changing Norms and Evolving Patterns in the Twentieth Century', in *China Report 33, Sage Publications, New Delhi.*

Rangaswami, S, 1995, 'Perspectives on The Indian State and its Discourse on Empowerment: The Issue of Power, State and Women's Mobilization', in *Vena Journal, Vol. 7 No.2.*

Rao, N, Rurup, L, and Sudarshan, R, 1995, *Sites of Change – The Structural Context for Empowering Women in India*, FES and UNDP, New Delhi.

Rao, V V B, 1998, 'East Asian Economies: The Crisis of 1997–98', in *Economic and Political Weekly, June 6th*

Robb, C M, 1998, 'Social Aspects of the East Asian Financial Crisis: Perceptions of Poor Communities' Paper Prepared for the *IDS East Asian Crisis Workshop, July 13 to 14th 1998*, Institute of Development Studies, England.

Rocheleau, D E, 1995, 'Gender and Biodiversity: A Feminist Political Ecology Perspective', in *Gender Relations and Environmental Change, Vol. 26 No.1.*

Rohde, J, Chatterjee, M, and Morley, D (eds.), 1993, *Reaching Health for All*, Oxford University Press, New Delhi.

Rosa, K, 1994, 'The Conditions and Organisational Activities of Women in Free Trade Zones – Malaysia, Philippines and Sri Lanka, 1970–1990', in Rowbotham, S, and Mitter, S (eds.), *Dignity and Daily Bread: New Forms of Economic Organizing Among Poor Women in the Third World and the First*, Women of South Asia, Gala Academic Press and Stiftung, Sri Lanka.

Roy, P, 1998, 'Sanctioned Violence: Development and Persecution of Women as Witches in South Bihar', in *Development in Practice, Vol. 8 No.2*.

Rudnick, A, 1996, *Foreign Labour in Malaysian Manufacturing*, INSAN, Kuala Lampur.

S

Sachs, A, 1993, 'Child Prostitution – The Asian Reality', in *Link Vol. 13 No.2*.

Sacks, R G, 1997, 'Commercial Sex and the Single Girl: Women's Empowerment Through Economic Development in Thailand', in *Development in Practice, Vol. 7 No.4*.

Safilios-Rothschild, C, 1991, 'Gender and Rural Poverty in Asia: Implications for Agricultural Project Design and Implementation', in *Asia–Pacific Journal of Rural Development, Vol. 1 No.1, July*.

Samarasinghe, N, 1997, 'Women's Participation in the Electoral Process of Sri Lanka', in *Forum News, Vol. 10 No.1*.

Sandbergen L S, 1995, *Women and Seasonal Labour Migration: Indo-Dutch Studies on Development Alternatives*, Sage Publications, New Delhi.

Sandhya, V, 1995, *Environment, Development and the Gender Gap*, Sage Publications, New Delhi.

Sarin, M, 1995, 'Regenerating India's Forests: Reconciling Gender Equity with Joint Forest Management', in *Gender Relations and Environmental Change, Vol. 26 No.1*.

Schuler, S R, Hashemi, S M, and Badal, S H, 1998, 'Men's Violence Against Women in Rural Bangladesh: Undermined or Exacerbated by Microcredit Programmes?', in *Development in Practice, Vol. 8 No.2*.

Schuler, S R, Hashemi, S M, and Riley, A P, 1997, 'The Influence of Women's Changing Roles and Status in Bangladesh's Fertility Transition: Evidence from a Study of Credit Programs and Contraceptive Use', in *World Development, Vol. 25 No.4*.

SEARCH, 1998, *Special Bulletin on Female Infanticide*, SEARCH, Bangalore.

Sen, A, 1998, 'Economic Reforms, Employment and Poverty Trends and Options', Paper Issued at the International Conference on *Poverty Emerging Challenges*, Organised by Bangladesh Institute of Development Studies held on 9–11th February, Dhaka, Bangladesh.

Sen, A K, 1981, *Poverty and Famines: An Essay on Entitlement and Deprivation*, Clarendon Press, Oxford.

–, 1990, 'Gender and Co-Operative Conflicts', in I Tinker (ed.) *Persistent Inequalities, Women and World Development*, Oxford University Press, New York and Oxford.

–, 1996, 'Radical Needs and Moderate Reforms', in Dreze and Sen (Eds.), *Indian Development: Selected Regional Perspectives*, Oxford University Press, New Delhi.

Sen, B, 1997, 'Politics of Poverty Alleviation', in *The Crisis of Governance – A Review of Bangladesh's Development*, Edited by Soban, R, Dhaka.

Sen, G, 1997, *Globalisation in the 21st Century: Challenges for Civil Society*, The Uva Development Lecture, delivered at The University of Amsterdam, June 20th, 1997, Institute for Development Research, Amsterdam.

Sen, G, and Heyzer, N, 1994, *Gender, Economic Growth and Poverty – Market Growth and State Planning in Asia and the Pacific*, APDC, Malaysia.

Sen, K, 1995, 'Gender, Culture, and Later Life: A Dilemma for Contemporary Feminism', in *Gender and Development, Vol. 3 No.3*.

Sen, P, 1996, 'Networks, Support Groups, and Domestic Violence', in *Development in Practice, Vol. 6 No.4*.

Shah, M K, and Shah, P, 1995, 'Gender, Environment and Livelihood Security: An Alternative Viewpoint from India', in *Gender Relations and Environmental Change, Vol. 26 No.1*.

Shah, N, Gothoskar, S, Gandhi, N, and Chhachhi, A, 1994, 'Structural Adjustment, Feminisation of Labour Force and Organisational Strategies', in *Economic and Political Weekly, Vol XXIX No.18*.

Bibliography

Sharma, C, 1996, *Coastal Area Management in South Asia: A Comparative Perspective*, International Collective in Support of Fishworkers, Chennai.

Sharma, C, 1998, *Changing Roles and Status of Women in Fishing Communities*, International Collective in Support of Fishworkers, Chennai.

Shaw, L, 1996, 'Report on a Conference: World Trade is a Women's Issue', in *Focus on Gender, Vol. 4 No.3*.

Shiva, V, 1996, *Globalisation of Agriculture and the Growth of Food Insecurity*, Research Foundation for Science, Technology and Ecology, New Delhi.

Slim, H, 1997, 'Relief Agencies and Moral Standing in War: Principles of Humanity, Neutrality, Impartiality, and Solidarity', in *Development in Practice, Vol. 7 No.4*.

Smith, W (Ed), 1997, Gender Impact Assessment for Workshop on 'Micro – Finance Programmes and Women's Empowerment: Strategies for Increasing Impact', ACTIONAID, Bangalore.

Smyth, I, 1995, 'Gender, Change, and Insecurity: Theoretical Issues and Practical Concerns', in *Gender and Development, Vol. 3 No.3*.

Specter, M, 1994, 'For Armenians, The War is Forever', in *THE INDEPENDENT, 23rd July*, Mumbai.

Spray, P, 1995, 'The World Bank's Poverty Strategy', in *Development and Practice, Vol. 5 No.1*.

Srinivasan, K, 1994, 'Sex Ratios: What They Reveal and What They Hide', *Economic and Political Weekly, Vol. XXIX Nos. 51–52*.

Stephens, A, 1995a, *Gender Issue in Agricultural and Rural Development Policy in Asia and The Pacific*, Regional Office for The Asia and Pacific, FAO, Bangkok.

Stephens, A, 1995b, 'Women Farmers' Worsening World: Can Gender Analysis Help?', in *Asia-Pacific Journal of Rural Development, Vol. V No.1*.

Stewart, F, 1996, 'Adjustment and Poverty: Options and Choices', in *Development in Practice, Vol. 6 No.1*.

Stewart, F, and Ranis, G, 1998, 'The Asian Crisis and Human Development', Paper Prepared for The IDS Seminar on *The Asian Crisis, July 13–14th, 1998*, Institute of Development Studies, United Kingdom.

Streeten P, 1995, 'The Framework of ILO Action Against Poverty', in *The Poverty Agenda and The ILO: Issues for Research and Action*, ILO, Geneva.

Stuart, S, 1996, 'Female-Headed Families: A Comparative Perspective of The Caribbean and The Developed World', in *Gender and Development, Vol. 4 No.2*.

Suryanarayana, M H, 1997, 'Uruguay Round and Global Food Security', in *Economic and Political Weekly, Vol. XXXII No. 43 Oct 25–31*.

T

Tantiwiramanond, D, 1997, 'Changing Gender Relations in Thailand: A Historical and Cultural Analysis', in *Indian Journal for Gender Studies 4:2*, Sage Publishers, New Delhi.

The Moscow Center for Gender Studies, 1996, *Report on The Legal Status of Women in Russia: Contemporary Debates*, Network of East-West Women Project, The Moscow Center for Gender Studies, Moscow.

Theobald, S, 1996, 'Employment and Environmental Hazard: Women Workers and Strategies of Resistance in Northern Thailand', in *Gender and Development, Vol. 4 No.3*.

Thi, L, 1995, 'Rural Women and The National Renovation Process in Vietnam', in *Asia-Pacific Journal of Rural Development, Vol. V No.1*.

Thitiprasert, W B, 1997, 'Women's Rights Situation in Thailand', *Friends of Women Newsletter, Vol. 8 Jan–Dec*, Bangkok.

Thompson, M, 1996,'Empowerment and Survival: Humanitarian Work in Civil Conflict (Part1)', in *Development in Practice, Vol. 6 No.4.*

Thorbek, S, 1994, *Gender and Slum Culture in Urban Asia*, Vistaar Publishers, New Delhi.

Timsina, D, Timsina, J, and Chhetry, N B, 1989,'Women's Role in Nepalese Farming Systems: A Comparative Study of a Hill and an Inner Terai Farming Systems Site', in *Working Paper 193, Michigan State University, USA*

Tinker, A, Daly, P, Green, C, Saxenian, H, Lakshminarayanan, R, and K, Gill, 1994,'Women's Health and Nutrition-Making a Difference', in *World Bank Discussion Paper No. 256*, World Bank, Washington DC.

U

Ul Haq, M, and Haq, K, 1998, *Human Development in South Asia 1998*, Oxford University Press, Karachi.

UN Department of Public Information, 1996, *The Beijing Declaration and The Platform for Action*, UN Department of Public Information, New York.

United Nations, 1994, Concept for *The Improvement of The Status of Women in The Russian Federation*, Concept Paper-Discussed and Approved at The National Conference on Women and Development, Moscow, Division for The Advancement of Women, UN.

–, 1995, *The Role of Women in United Nations Peace-Making*, United Nations Division for the Advancement of Women, DPCSD, United Nations.

–, 1996, *Rural Poverty Alleviation and Sustainable Development in Asia and the Pacific*, Economic and Social Commission for Asia and the Pacific, United Nations, New York

UNAIDS, 1997, Proceedings of an Official Satellite Symposium IV International Conference on *AIDS in Asia and the Pacific*, Manila, Oct 25–27, UNAIDS

UNDP, 1990, *Human Development Report*, Oxford University Press, New York.

–, 1995, *Human Development Report*, Oxford University Press, New York

–, 1997, *Human Development Report*, Oxford University Press, New York.

–, 1998, *Human Development Report*, Oxford University Press, New York

UNFPA, 1997, *The State of World Population*, Prographics Inc., U S A.

UNHCR, 1997, *Update on Regional Developments in Asia and the Pacific*, UNHCR, Switzerland.

UNICEF, 1996, *Atlas of South Asian Children and Women*, UNICEF Regional Office for South Asia, Nepal.

UNIFEM, 1995, *The Human Costs of Women's Poverty: Perspectives from Latin America and the Caribbean*, United Nations Office, Mexico

Uphoff, N, 1993,'Grassroots Organisations and NGOs In Rural Development: Opportunities with Diminishing States and Expending Markets', in *World Development, Vol. 21 No. 4.*

V

Venkateshwaran, S, 1995, *Environment, Development and the Gender Gap*, Sage Publications, New Delhi.

Verma, A S, and Singh, A K, 1996, *BHUTAN Tek Nath Rizal & Struggle for Democracy*, issued in Solidarity with Democratic Movement of Bhutan by Bhutan Solidarity, India.

Voluntary Health Association of India, 1997, *ANUBHAV: Health Promotion in South-East Asia*, VHAI, New Delhi.

W

Wade, R, and White, G,1984,'Development States in East Asia: Capitalist and Socialist', *IDS Bulletin, Vol. 15 No.2.*

Wahab, F R, 1995,'Is Women's Loan Repayment Behaviour Different Than Men's? An Analysis of Gender Differentials in Loan Repayment in Four CIRDAP Member Countries', in *Asia-Pacific Journal of Rural Development, Vol. V No.1.*

Walter, V, 1996, 'Focusing on Women and Poverty Alleviation', in *Attacking The Roots of Poverty, Series A-13*, Marburg Consult For Self-Help Promotion, Marburg, Germany.

Watkins, K, 1995, *The Oxfam Poverty Report*, Oxfam, UK.

Watkins, K, 1998, *Economic Growth with Equity – Lessons From East Asia*, Oxfam Oxford.

Weizhan, D, 1996,'Urban Women's Employment and Unemployment in an Age of Transition from State-Led to Market-Led Economy – A Case Study of Shangai, China', *Working Paper Series No.222*, Institute of Social Studies, Netherlands.

White, H, 1996,'How Much Aid is Used for Poverty Reduction?', in *IDS Bulletin Vol. 27 No.1.*

Wieringa, S,1995, 'The Indonesian Women's Movement Gerwani and the Change from Sukarno's Old Order to Suharto's New Order', in *Vena Journal, Vol. 7 No.2.*

Wignaraja, P, 1990, *Women, Poverty and Resources*, Sage Publishers, New Delhi.

Wils, F, and Acharya, S K,1997, *Promoting Self-Reliance of the Rural Poor in India*, ISSAS, Netherlands.

Women's Feature Service, 1992, *The Power to Change – Women in the Third World Redefine Their Environment*, Zed Books Ltd, London.

Women's Rights Watch, 1998, *Women's Rights Watch – 1st Quarter 1998*, Women and Media Collective, Colombo.

Women Watch,1995,'Kyrgyzstan National Plan of Action 1997–2000', in *Fourth World Conference on Women, Beijing.*

World Bank Policy Research Report, 1997, *Confronting Aids – Public Priorities in a Global Epidemic*, Oxford University Press Inc.,

World Bank, 1990, *World Development Report*, Oxford University Press, New York.

–, 1994, *Enhancing Women's Participation in Economic Development: A World Bank Policy Paper*, World Bank, Washington.

–, 1995a, *World Development Report: 1995, Workers in an Integrating World*, World Bank, Washington.

–,1995b, *Advancing Gender Equality – From Concept to Action*, The World Bank Publication, Washington DC.

–, 1995c, *Cambodia: Country Gender Profile*, Gender and Poverty Team, Asia Technical Human Resources, The World Bank, Washington.

–, 1995d, *China: Country Gender Profile*, Gender and Poverty Team, Asia Technical Human Resources, The World Bank, Washington.

–, 1995e, *Indonesia: Country Gender Profile*, Gender and Poverty Team, Asia Technical Human Resources, The World Bank, Washington.

–, 1995f, *Malaysia: Country Gender Profile*, Gender and Poverty Team, Asia Technical Human Resources, The World Bank, Washington.

–, 1995g, *Mongolia: Country Gender Profile*, Gender and Poverty Team, Asia Technical Human Resources, The World Bank, Washington.

–, 1995h, *Philippines: Country Gender Profile*, Gender and Poverty Team, Asia Technical Human Resources, The World Bank, Washington.

–, 1995i, *Thailand: Country Gender Profile*, Gender and Poverty Team, Asia Technical Human Resources, The World Bank, Washington.

–, 1995j, *Vietnam: Country Gender Profile*, Gender and Poverty Team, Asia Technical Human Resources, The World Bank, Washington.

–, 1996b, *Bhutan: Profile of Women in Agriculture*, Gender and Poverty Team, Asia Technical Human Resources, The World Bank, Washington.

–, 1996c, *Cambodia: Profile of Women in Agriculture*, Gender and Poverty Team, Asia Technical Human Resources, The World Bank, Washington.

–, 1996d, *China: Profile of Women in Agriculture*, Gender and Poverty Team, Asia Technical Human Resources, The World Bank, Washington.

–, 1996e, *Indonesia: Profile of Women in Agriculture*, Gender and Poverty Team, Asia Technical Human Resources, The World Bank, Washington.

–, 1996f, *India: Profile of Women in Agriculture*, Gender and Poverty Team, Asia Technical Human Resources, The World Bank, Washington.

–, 1996g, *Lao PDR: Profile of Women in Agriculture*, Gender and Poverty Team, Asia Technical Human Resources, The World Bank, Washington.

–, 1996h, *Mongolia: Profile of Women in Agriculture*, Gender and Poverty Team, Asia Technical Human Resources, The World Bank, Washington.

–, 1996i, *Nepal: Profile of Women in Agriculture*, Gender and Poverty Team, Asia Technical Human Resources, The World Bank, Washington.

–, 1996j, *Pakistan: Profile of Women in Agriculture*, Gender and Poverty Team, Asia Technical Human Resources, The World Bank, Washington.

–, 1996k, *Philippines: Profile of Women in Agriculture*, Gender and Poverty Team, Asia Technical Human Resources, The World Bank, Washington.

–, 1996l, *Sri Lanka: Profile of Women in Agriculture*, Gender and Poverty Team, Asia Technical Human Resources, The World Bank, Washington.

–, 1996m, *Thailand: Profile of Women in Agriculture*, Gender and Poverty Team, Asia Technical Human Resources, The World Bank, Washington.

–, 1996n, *Vietnam: Profile of Women in Agriculture*, Gender and Poverty Team, Asia Technical Human Resources, The World Bank, Washington.

–, 1997a, *Poverty Reduction and The World Bank-Progress in Fiscal 1996 and 1997*, The World Bank, Washington D C.

–, 1997b, *World Development Report – The State in a Changing World*, Oxford University Press, New York.

–, 1998a, *World Development Indicators*, The World Bank, Washington DC.

–, 1998b, *Responding to the Crisis: Backing East Asia's Social and Financial Reforms*, World Bank, Washington.

Y

Yasmin, T, 1993, 'Saptagram Opens Up Windows of Opportunity in Bangladesh' in *Focus on Gender, Vol. 1 No.3*.

Ykhanbai, H, 1996, *Economic Incentives for Environment and Sustainable Development in Mongolia and Central Asia*, Ministry of Nature and The Environment, Mongolia.

Z

Zanna, J, 1997, 'CEDAW Watch In Mongolia', in *Asia Pacific Forum on Women, Law and Development, Vol. 10 No.2*.

Zwarteven, M, and Neupane, N, 1995, 'Gender Aspects of Irrigation Management: The Chhattis Mauja Irrigation System in Nepal', in *Asia-Pacific Journal of Rural Development, Vol. V No.1*, Somporn Hanpongpandh, Bangladesh.